Scribing the Soul

Kathleen Adams

ESSAYS IN JOURNAL THERAPY

by Kathleen Adams LPC, RPT
Director, Center for Journal Therapy

with poetry by Amy Christman

Center for Journal Therapy
1115 Grant Street, Suite 207
Denver CO 80203
888-421-2298   303-986-6460
www.journaltherapy.com

First publishing credits. All material © Kathleen Adams.

The Art of Conscious Co-Creation, SoulfulLiving.com, January 2003
Pockets of Joy, SoulfulLiving.com, July 2000
Scribing the Authentic Self, Mightier Than the Sword (1994, Warner Books)
Soul Food, SoulfulLiving.com, October 2000
Journals to Go, Journal to the Self (1990, Warner Books)
Writing in the Dark, SoulfulLiving.com, July 2001
Families Writing, SoulfulLiving.com, November 2001
Life Story Writing for Seniors, Journal of Certified Senior Advisors, Vol. IX,
   January 2000
Love Letters, SoulfulLiving.com, February 2001
And All is Well: Jihan's Story, Healing Touch Hawaii newsletter, Fall 2000
Diary of a Headache, SoulfulLiving.com, September 2000
Making Up the Truth, SoulfulLiving.com, August 2000
Managing Grief Through Journal Writing, The MADDvocate, January 2001
Coping Strategies for Catastrophic Trauma, Center for Journal Therapy handout,
   September 2001
Journal of a Synchronicity, SoulfulLiving.com, September 2001
Five Ways to Scribe Your Intuition, SoulfulLiving.com, June 2000
Riding the Inky Wave, SoulfulLiving.com, December 2000
Unseen Companions, SoulfulLiving.com, December 2001
Saying Goodbye, Saying Hello, Center for Journal Therapy handout, December 2003

Published by the Center for Journal Therapy, 1115 Grant Street #207, Denver CO 80203,
www.journaltherapy.com.

International Standard Book Number 0-9676552-4-2

Cover design, page design, layout and typography by Mary Caprio (mfcaprio@comcast.net)

To Dana,

precious friend,

who teaches me the art of soulful living

In ancient times, scribes were devotees of the Word.
They were the bridges between worlds,
charged with the sacred task of painstakingly transcribing the Mysteries
into a form that could be referenced by holy men and women.
Many centuries later, our modern journals give us unlimited access
to the Mysteries of our souls. These essays,
offerings to the Word,
invite us to approach our own lives
with the love and devotion of the scribes of old.

Scribing the Soul

ESSAYS IN JOURNAL THERAPY
by Kathleen Adams

with poetry by Amy Christman

Illness, Trauma, and Recovery

Intuition and Spirituality

Saying Goodbye, Saying Hello

Sea Change

I let go of certainties the way a wave
lets go of shore, knowing it will soon
return, knowing that even in the long
retreat back into the sea, there is building
the momentum for another trip home.
All my life I have stored missed opportunities,
wrong words, or the right ones withheld,
let them gather in long gnarled strands
like seaweed hunched on the shore,
a barrier to letting go and moving forward.
I have listened to voices uttering bad advice,
like the sass of gulls screeching "failure," and
"hopeless," I have snapped and twisted,
useless as a ripped sail under the flexed
muscle of wind, the rasping presence
of bodies stronger than my own. Stray
grit blown between my teeth sharpens them,
my tongue returning again and again to those
jagged edges, making of them an altar, brilliant
and lacey as coral, touched by the light of my
knowing that rescue can be swift and sudden
as riptide, the frothy tumult of turning away
from what is known, carried beyond the
fringe of breaking waves, the deep dive
into open water on its way to a new shore.

Amy Christman

Introduction

I write these words in early springtime, at my mahogany desk overlooking the flower garden I dearly love. Tulips, daffodils and crocus start their annual push upward toward the light, and soon they will be joined by plump peonies, daisies, marigolds, iris, roses, stock and yarrow. For the next eight months I will gladly gather armloads of flowers and bring them indoors to arrange, tossing color and texture and aroma together in bright welcome.

The essays in this collection are akin to my garden arrangements. They each began as something else: An article for a magazine, a column for a website, a chapter in a book. Separately, they are as stand-alone as a single stem of tea rose. Assembled, they make a bouquet that I dare to hope is fresh and fragrant.

Most of these essays were first published in the e-zine *Soulful Living*, where for nearly two years I wrote a monthly column called "Scribing the Soul." I am grateful to Valerie Rickel, founder and publisher of *Soulful Living,* for her enthusiastic response when I first suggested gathering my columns together in a collection.

The concept for this book didn't really take off, however, until I hit upon the idea of asking my friend and poetry therapy colleague Amy Christman to contribute some of her original poems to accompany the essays. Amy is a fresh and exciting voice in the poetry therapy movement, and I am thrilled to be the first publisher of her work.

Amy sent me a sheaf of 22 of what she considered her best poems. It soon became clear that we had an uncanny fit (as she said, *spooky cool*), and all but two of the poems she sent are included. I matched poems with essays to reinforce or amplify themes, and each poem includes a writing suggestion that I have crafted to extend the essay's journal writing prompts into poetry writing. Since poetry comes alive when it is voiced, when it is given breath, I encourage you to read Amy's poems out loud, more than once.

I hope the essays and poems in this collection, like my garden blossoms, bring immediate beauty to your life. Even more, I hope that they help you grow sturdy roots of meaning, and inspire you to scatter seeds of possibility.

Kathleen Adams
March 2004

CHAPTER 1

The Art of Conscious Co-Creation

I am often asked how I became one of the pioneers of the movement known as journal therapy. How did I enter into this work in 1985, when there were precious few footprints to step into and follow?

The answer is simple, and also complex. I followed God's instructions for my life, as revealed through tragedy, synchronicity and Mystery.

From the time I was a small girl I was aware of synchronicity. I didn't have a name for it then, but it absorbed me when I climbed up into the wide arms of the pear tree in our back yard. I thought about my sense that things didn't just happen without reason, meaning or connection. In a way that I could not begin to articulate, I was certain that all the circumstances of my life were closely intertwined and meaningful. Why was I born into this family, with this mom and dad and sister? Why did I live next door to this best friend? Why did my dog get run over by a car? Why did my three-years-elder sister (who now holds a doctorate in elementary education) teach me to read when I was only three, causing my teacher to boot me out of first grade? The only sense I could make of it, sitting in the treehouse my father built, was that these experiences, the painful and the pleasant, were necessary preludes to some future I could only imagine.

I remember feeling comforted by this awareness at the same time that it confounded me, and I especially remember the palpable presence of intuition in that pear tree, whispering assurances that yes, what I pondered would all come to be revealed.

Fast forward to adolescence. My clear channels of connection to my intuitive self got buried under pubescent hormones, and my wise child surrendered to a teenager who valued boyfriends more than angel friends. Fast forward through college, where social activism, campus protests and peace rallies took precedence over the inner life, and where no higher meaning whatsoever could be made of the killing fields of Viet Nam. Fast forward through my 20s and a failed marriage, a whirlwind courtship, a second marriage, and a promising career as a professional writer. Fast forward to the age of 31, when I suddenly and startlingly became a widow.

The event more than 20 years ago that resulted in my husband's death was a tragedy, and I came out of it irrevocably changed. In the trauma of that time, all the wisdom of my childhood poured back into me, and I became undeniably clear that Spirit and Soul were partnered in a timeless dance of meaning and purpose. I came to the other side of that experience knowing at my core that I had been given back my interior life, and without any hesitation at all I turned it over to God, trusting that I would be guided to the people, places and situations that would lead to fulfillment of my highest purpose and destiny.

In 20-plus years, I have never doubted this, nor have I been disappointed.

Only days after the awful event that ended my husband's life, at the strong urging of my minister, I found myself in a modified Intensive Journal Workshop® led by Eiko Michi, a former colleague of Dr. Ira Progoff (who I consider to be the founder of the movement I later called journal therapy). I had no idea that people who weren't professional writers wrote journals; I had always assumed that I was a lifelong journaler because I was a lifelong writer. The awareness that others also took solace and comfort in writing was a profound discovery.

Equally profound was the guidance I received when my writer's journal became specifically focused on my interior life. Starting with that landmark workshop experience, I realized that through my journal I could consciously and intentionally enter into co-creative partnership with the Divine. I began to recognize my journal as the incubator for the laboratory of my life. For a while I experimented with a sort of spiritual "name it and claim it" game, where I wrote in specific detail what I wanted to create or manifest, and then carefully logged the synchronicities and serendipities that drew me to the outcomes I desired. As I matured I learned how to balance the clear, focused statement of my own will with the surrender of my will to Divine Will.

Three years after that first Progoff workshop I received an unmistakeable "message" to teach a journal writing class. The "messenger" was a friend who casually mentioned that she and others in our circle had a hard time getting started and staying with this journal thing. Could I offer some pointers? The message, however, was from God, and it was the first time I consciously took into my journal a co-creative endeavor that did not originate from my personality self.

God did God's part. The curriculum and processes for what became the Journal to the Self® workshop flowed through me as if I were taking dictation. I would pose a question to myself, sit with it until the urge to write began, and then flow out the answer. Today, the Journal to the Self workshop is still taught essentially the way it presented itself to me in 1985. It remains one of the most consistently viable models for teaching a variety of writing techniques, designed to produce specific outcomes in a personal growth or therapeutic context. (**For brief descriptions of all the techniques referenced in this book, turn to page 149 and read "Journal Toolbox."**)

I taught the first class over a four-week time frame to a group of seven friends who sat on my living room floor and wrote their hearts out. I knew instantaneously that this was the work I was put on the planet to do. Following that pull, I taught the basic class, along with many variations and adaptations that I developed, more than 100 times in the next three years. I was also a graduate student in counseling psychology in those years, and I taught myself how to parallel my emerging work in journal therapy with the clinical skills and theoretical understanding I was cultivating in grad school. Then one snowy day I sat down at my IBM typewriter and rolled in a fresh piece of paper. Several hours later I had a stack of pages next to me. It seemed undeniably like the first two chapters of a book.

I wrote *Journal to the Self* in three phases. The first phase was two weeks of nonstop writing over winter semester break, my last year of graduate school. It netted 100 fresh, finished pages that sold on first submission to Warner Books. Then a long dry spell occurred, during which I choked out a few pages every now and then. I began to doubt whether or not I could pull this off. My journals were fat with anguished writes about self-sabotage. Consistently I wrote my inner wisdom's response: "Just wait. It's not time yet. Be patient." Impatiently I practiced patience, and the day finally came when I shut myself in my "office" (in those days I was writing in the laundry room) and didn't come out for eight days or nights except for naps and snacks. I spent the next month revising, and I submitted the completed manuscript by September deadline.

Journal to the Self: 22 Paths to Personal Growth was released January 1, 1990 to immediate critical acclaim. I received my first reader mail within two weeks of its release. The reader was a 17-year-old girl who told me she used *Journal to the Self* to start a journal about her ongoing sexual abuse. Within three entries she had the courage to hand the notebook to her mother, who immediately packed up the children and left the stepfather. The second letter was from a research librarian on Long Island, Lisa Shumicky, who has since become legendary among the journal community for her devotion to all things journal. More letters from readers followed, each telling a story of triumph over despair, discovery of unknown resources, clarity of vision, increased possibilities. Fifteen years after the initial publication of *Journal to the Self,* I am still receiving letters and emails in which people tell me their stories. I consider them a high privilege and honor, and I read and try to answer every one.

It was about this time, when *Journal to the Self* began to make its way into the world, that I deeply acknowledged that Soul, Spirit and I were in a constant covenant, a voluntary and sacred commitment. I once again dedicated my life and my work to God. I make this rededication every day, and I formally ritualize the rededication each year on November 5, the anniversary of the first *Journal to the Self* workshop. This covenant is the heart of my spiritual practice. It guides my daily life. There are times when it is not easy, but it is always interesting, and mostly it is joyful. I have been given wonderful work to do, and wonderful people to do it with. Consciously co-creating my life with Soul and Spirit is the greatest adventure I can imagine.

Starting Over

I am starting over.
My life is not my own
in the way that hotel rooms
are comfortable,
even sometimes pretty
but not a place to call home.
I have been a visitor
these thirty-eight years,
polite
quiet
staying in the shadows
out of the way.

I am starting over.
I am not moving to a new house
or changing my name.
I am keeping my job
which I wear
like an old coat, familiar
and wearing at the seams.

I am starting over,
starting up,
starting out
with words and attitudes new
and sweet as June's first berries.
I wear the juice on my
chin, without apology,

and suck the sweetness on my tongue
feeling smug and sated with this
life I have claimed
and will someday
own.

Starting over
sometimes means giving up
or letting go,
and sometimes
it means holding on hard,
but mostly it means I get
another chance, this time
to do it
right.

Amy Christman

Write a poem that begins with and repeats the line,
"I am starting over...."

PERSONAL GROWTH

CHAPTER 2

Pockets of Joy

I remember as magical the blazing hot Julys of my middle child-hood. The school year just past was a distant memory; the school year to come was in the far future. My suburban neighborhood, once fertile farmland, was friendly, safe and slow-paced. I'd mount my bike in early light and roam the creeks and cottonwood thickets until hunger drove me homeward. After lunch, I'd do it again.

I was a collector of all things interesting and random: Seedpods, rocks, shriveled cocoons, squashed pennies, bottle caps, pencil stubs. All of it got crammed into the pockets of my shorts. These were also the summers my mother taught me to do laundry, so once a week I'd dump my shorts and tops into the washer and pour in a cup of Tide, mindless of the trail of debris I left behind.

My mother's task was to rescue her washing machine from the flotsam and jetsam of my travels. "I see you've got pockets of joy again," she'd say wryly, reaching deep into the basin to retrieve my treasures.

My carefree Julys are gone, but I've carried forward some habits: I'm still a wanderer, I'm still a gatherer, and I still seek pockets of joy to surprise and delight me. Here are four ways I create pockets of joy in my journal.

1. **Treat your journal like a scrapbook.** Buy a 3-pack of gluesticks and keep one in your purse or briefcase, one in your stash place at work, and one in your favorite journal spot at home. (If you keep one in the car, make sure it's in a baggie in case it melts.) Now you are free to paste in mementos of your daily wanderings: A comic strip or cartoon that tickles your funny-bone, a movie ticket stub, your fortune cookie fortune, the photocopied lyrics to your favorite song from your new CD, a post card from the country inn where you had Sunday brunch with out-of-town friends. Writing about the event is optional. There's not a word in my journal about thrill and delight at the stage production of *The Lion King,* but my glued-in ticket stub is an instant return.

2. **Log your joy.** Keep a Joy Log. Start by listing three pockets of joy in every day. Anything counts that brings a smile to your eyes, a lift to your heart or a stirring to your soul — a sunset, the laughter of a child, an answered prayer, feeling at home in your body, the scent of roses in your yard. As you develop the habit of joy, expand your repertoire to five daily joys, or even ten. Or you can borrow a spiritual practice from Brother David Steindl-Rast, who strives to find one new thing each and every day to praise. He says he was worried at first that he might run out of fresh ways to be surprised, delighted and grateful, but it hasn't happened yet.

3. **Delight in sensory details.** Indulge in the pleasures of the sensual, sensory world. Take time to fully appreciate the taste

and texture of an exquisite piece of exactly ripe fruit. Breathe in the luscious smells of seasons: Burgers on the grill; crisp leaves; evergreens; April rains. Put on music that transports you back to a carefree, joyful time in your life. Write about your joy.

4. **Capture a moment of joy.** The Captured Moments journal technique is a short vignette that freezes a moment of time permanently in prose, just as a camera shutter capture a moment of time on film. Captured Moments are characterized by their intensity of description. This is a place to allow yourself to use all the luscious, rich, evocative images, adjectives and verbs that you can call forth. Choose something from your Joy Log — a moment of pure, unadulterated joy, beauty or bliss — and write about it. Be flowery. Be intense. Be dramatic!

As a journal therapist who spends a good portion of every day working with people in pain, I know how easy and effective it is to turn to the journal as a never-ending friend in need. But any friendship needs balance. A little pocket of joy every now and then will go a long way toward bringing necessary balance to your journal. And your soul and spirit will thrive!

MOMENTS

There are moments sweet as nectar
on the back of the throat, the taste
of clover and honey, the scent of
rich earth and early mist.

Moments, slender and fleeting as
a flash of red wing against the
brush ends of dark pines.

There are moments that stand me still
as the etched gloss of ice on the
window, the bright slice of jet stream
in the blue carpet of sky,

Moments of heat that fill me with
the grace of a candle's fluid flame,
the dance and flicker of quiet awareness.

There are moments of pure color and
clarity that gather like wintering geese
along the edges of swift rivers,

Moments for which there is no other
use than the deep joy, the full
richness of abandon and grace.

Amy Christman

Poetry Prompt

List or Cluster the moments of any given day
or experience. Extend the moments by finding
a sensory word or phrase to describe them.

Write a poem that begins, "There are moments...."

CHAPTER 3

Scribing the Authentic Self[1]

The room was silent save for the faint hum of the heating system and the determined scratching of pens on notebooks. The group was noting observations made in a guided imagery process. *Imagine yourself doing something you really enjoy. Now imagine that an expert in human behavior watches you do it. Write the expert's observations.*

Midway through the writing time, Jerry drew a sharp breath and closed his notebook. He glanced over at me, and I saw that his eyes were filled with pain. He seemed to shrink inside his crisp white button-down shirt.

When the group finished writing, I turned to Jerry. "Anything you want to share?"

---

1 Originally published in *Mightier Than the Sword: The Journal as a Path to Men's Self-Discovery*, Warner Books, 1994. Copyright and publishing rights have reverted to the author. Although the masculine gender and case studies of men are used throughout this essay, concepts are equally applicable to both genders.

"This is fraudulent!" His voice shook with an ancient, tired bitterness. "I am nothing but a fraud!" And he read:

> *The image is of a "father figure" with all the correct yuppie attributes. The image is just that, an image. there is a distinct absence of BEING — in particular, being present to the joy at depth of a profound relationship with my daughter ... Who or what is the image being? What motivates the image to appear or be recognized? What conspiracies influence its identity? It would seem that most of them have very little to do with BEING a father and much more to do with BEING CONSTRUED as a father. What's authentic about this? Well, it seems to be an authentic polarity.*

"And what's fraudulent about this," he continued, "is that what I write is nothing like what I feel!"

The discrepancy between image/being, external/internal, acculturated self/authentic self — "the maintenance of the lie" — reverberates in the journals of men like an echo bouncing off of canyon walls. The search for authenticity is a modern-day grail quest. It is the beating heart of many men's writings.

In my office hangs a small mirror. To introduce the concept of authenticity, I ask the members of the group to look at themselves in the mirror and write down what they notice. This process is usually punctuated with some self-conscious joking as the group members wait in single-file line and then make faces, practice smiling and reluctantly meet their own eyes in the mirror. The writings are poignant and telling:

- *I'm getting older, but I still look good. I like my looks. I've matured. Maybe I also like how I am inside.*

- *Gray hair, thinning, "giant economy size" forehead. At least I didn't break the mirror! Good thing I couldn't see my paunch!*
- *This was harder than it sounded. I can barely look myself in the eye. What do I think I'll see? Reminds me of that poem about facing the man in the mirror each day. Spooky.*

The mirror on my wall reflects the outer man. The journal, as mirror of the psyche, captures the inner man. Stay with the journal process for even a little while and you'll start to see the layers of your life. You'll begin to hear the voices inside. Like the increasingly soft leaves in each layer of an artichoke, the journal peels off layers of conditioning, habits and worn-out beliefs and reveals the heart nestled snugly inside.

What is authenticity? The men speak:

> *Authenticity is.....*
> *...being real.*
> *...the REAL me. Not the one I show most of the time.*
> *...something I can't sustain for long.*
> *...honesty.*
> *...when who I am on the outside matches who I am on the inside.*
> *...genuine.*
> *....living instead of being a robot.*
> *...the real McCoy, natural, no bullshit.*
>
> *My authentic self...*
> *...is hidden,*
> *...is warm, loving, affectionate.*
> *...wants to get out of "jail."*
> *...?? I don't know my authentic self.*

...tells the truth even when I don't want to know it.
...hates my job.
...is my Inner Child.
...is mad at me.

Suggestions for Meeting Your Authentic Self

1. Complete these Sentence Stems:
   Authenticity is....
   My authentic self...
   I am....
   I am not....

2. Imagine that a newspaper or magazine reporter is interviewing
   you for a story. He or she asks you questions like:
   What habit would you most like to break?
   How did you meet your best friend?
   Which one year of your life would you live over again?
   Why?
   What do you consider your best attribute or feature?
   What did you want to be when you were a kid?
   If you won a lottery that allowed you a comfortable lifestyle,
   how would you spend your time?
   What is something very few people know about you?

3. As children, we were natural, instinctive, authentic and intuitive.
   Children adapt to their environments by layering over the
   authentic self, but it is and always has been there. Look back at
   your childhood joys and pleasures. What do you remember?

4. Cluster "authenticity" or "my authentic self."

5. Discovering the authentic self involves unraveling layers of the conditioned or acculturated self. Try a List of 100 on one of these topics. When you're finished, go through and break the list into categories.

   100 Roles I Play
   100 Ways I Fake It
   100 Beliefs I am Challenging
   100 Fears I Have About Being More Authentic
   100 Payoffs for Not Changing

6. What is one of your secrets? Who knows about this secret? Who do you wish knew? From whom is it a secret? What might happen if this secret were known? What good might come of it?

7. Think of somebody who only knows the public you. See yourself through this person's eyes. How would he or she describe you?

8. Imagine yourself doing something you really, truly love. Now imagine that an expert in human behavior known for his or her brilliant powers of observation watches you. What does he or she write in the report?

9. Explore a secret in your journal. When you're finished, read it once and tear it up.

10. Write about a peak experience — a time when you felt truly alive and authentic.

11. Take a walk somewhere in nature. Be on the lookout for an object or symbol from your walk that represents your authentic self. Write about it. Stay alert for serendipities or synchronicities involving your object/symbol. Keep track of them and write about what they might mean.

Because authenticity shares a boundary with exposure, working with authenticity issues can leave you feeling naked and vulnerable; and because the unmasked self is not silent, many a notebook is slammed shut when vulnerability kicks into high gear.

Remember to pace yourself. If you find yourself reluctant to pick up your journal, you may be going too fast. Take it easy. Write for shorter periods of time, or about less challenging topics. Feedback and support are very helpful. This work is powerful when it is done in a community of trusted others.

EVERYTHING I'VE EVER KNOWN

*What if you could remember everything that ever happened to you —
would it be a blessing, or a curse?*
from <u>Spilling Clarence: A Novel</u>, by Anne Ursu

Everything I've ever known is with me still,
bits of Kindergarten wedged between each toe,
High school banished to the shadows behind
my spine, womb pictures hung in rows along
the length of my thigh. Recent years cling
to the tips of my fingers like good dirt
gathered between thick garden rows.
Every place I've ever visited has dropped
a pebble in my pocket, history dripping like
tears from their thick skins. Everyone I've
ever loved breathes through my lungs.
Everything I've ever done still travels the
long road of my blood from heart to brain
and back. All of my life is hiding in this
imperfect body, waiting to be remembered
in a certain slant of light, the timbre of a voice,
the slow path of a hand, tilt of a head, curve
of shoulder or hip. Whole years gather
in the tatters of a song, faces swim in good
wine, rooms emerge from the scent of
flowers or spice. Blessing or curse,
everything I've ever known is with me,
and I am trying to remember all of it.

Amy Christman

Poetry Prompt

Notice how this poem is structured through a list of
body parts that hold specific types of memories.
Try your own list poem. Read this poem aloud, noticing
where you are particularly drawn by the imagery.
Start with that line and begin writing. For instance,
if you are drawn by the image of "whole years gather
in the tatters of a song," start your poem with that line.
Then list song titles or lyric lines and pair them
with your specific memories or experiences.

CHAPTER 4

Soul food:
Exploring Affirmations in Writing

We've all heard about affirmations: Powerful, positive statements, framed in the present tense, that speak the underlying truth about ourselves and our lives. It is commonly agreed that the ongoing repetition of affirmations can not only have a meditative, calming effect but can also have the power to dramatically shift our self-concept by moving us into "possibility thinking."

One of the best-kept secrets of affirmations, however, is the way they are amplified and constellated when they are explored in writing. Try this smorgasbord of 31 affirmations, one for each day of the month. Follow the calendar and use each day's affirmation as a writing prompt, or scan the list until you find one you want to explore deeply, and use it as a writing theme for a week or longer. May these affirmations richly feed your soul.

1. I now surrender all of my worries to the Divine as I experience it.

2. I view obstacles as lessons, not failures.

3. My needs are met perfectly by Infinite Intelligence.

4. I release my anger toward those who have hurt me.

5. This morning, I select my attitude for the day.

6. I am a beacon of love, light and peace.

7. I embrace gratitude.

8. I draw to myself people who appreciate my gifts and strengths.

9. I am whole, healthy and complete.

10. Grace goes before me, preparing the way.

11. I trust that I am in the right place at the right time.

12. All mistakes are opportunities to begin again, with added information.

13. I am on a path of true discovery.

14. I am open to the gifts and abundance of life.

15. I calmly and purposefully greet this day.

16. I am a smart, powerful, dynamic, capable, self-confident person.

17. Even in the midst of struggle, I can always choose the thoughts that enhance my life.

18. Whenever a difficult situation arises, answers come to me easily, and I immediately know what to do.

19. I have the freedom to choose my thoughts.

20. I allow all feelings in myself and others.

21. The still, small voice within me grows clearer and stronger each day.

22. My life is rich in ways that I have only just begun to understand.

23. Abundance is all around me, and I openly accept it.

24. I cherish myself, in exactly the package I come in.

25. I surrender my will to Divine Will.

26. My mind is alert, clear and aware. I know everything I need to know, when I need to know it.

27. I am deeply rooted.

28. My freedom is always available to me. I refuse bondage.

29. I harmonize with the new, higher awareness that resonates within me.

30. I courageously lean into my next step.

31. All is well with my soul.

When this essay first appeared in *Soulful Living*, Mary Lee printed out all 31 affirmations and taped them into her journal. She used each daily affirmation as a writing prompt. On the 18th of the month she experienced a sudden, frightening heart condition. Keeping in mind her morning write on the topic, "Whenever a difficult situation arises, answers come to me easily, and I immediately know what to do," she took appropriate emergency action and was admitted to the intensive care unit for heart monitoring. Throughout the coming days, she continued her daily writes while under the care of a doctor who was not philosophically aligned with her preferred treatment strategies. While writing on the topic of "The still, small voice within me grows clearer and stronger each day," Mary Lee found the courage to confront her doctor and hire a different cardiologist.

This dramatic story underscores the basic premise of journal therapy that we do indeed know more than we may consciously understand or remember, and writing brings this underlying wisdom to our awareness, where it can be accessed and used. It's such a simple practice. And its outcomes, literally or metaphorically, can help save your life.

THIS MANTLE OF SKY

I pull this mantle of dark clouds around me,
tuck the corners neatly up under my feet,
across my shoulders, snugly up under
my chin. The weight of this rough blanket
holds me inside my skin. There is the urge
to abandon all control, to howl and sing,
dance naked under this roiling sky. My grief
glows like leaves heated to hues of smoldering
embers. I want to turn myself inside out,
become empty and hollow as milkweed husk,
spill my bitter seeds into brisk wind and watch
them scatter. I spread cold hands over my
tight belly, expecting the slippery heat of blood
and entrails, find only the soft down of my own
small life. I pull this mantle of sky around me,
remember the heat scent of wind dried sheets,
almost remember your voice calling me to
breakfast. The stitches that bind us together
are loose, but the thread is strong. I pull the
blanket of your love around me, tuck the
corners neatly under my feet, across my
shoulders, snugly up under my chin.

Amy Christman

An affirmation is particularly powerful when it can help reframe a difficult circumstance or limiting belief. Notice how the poet's perspective on her grief shifts as she moves closer and closer to affirmative language by the end of the poem. Her final statement, "I pull the blanket of your love around me," has transformed the opening line into an affirmation. Write an opening line that describes a difficult or painful situation in your life, and through poetic language allow it to transform.

CHAPTER 5

Journals to Go:
15 Ways to Write for Under 15 Minutes Each²

I gave up chocolate. I gave up espresso. I gave up the Count
(that naughty man) and his little house in Cap Ferrat.
This Waterman, however, is not negotiable. I must have
something thrilling with which to record my boredom.
—Waterman Pen Company advertisement

Ah yes, the boredom. It's easy enough to find time for melancholy introspection when there's nothing else to do. But what about those languid nights of chocolate, conversation and espresso? What about the times when that scoundrel, the Count, is whisking you off to Cap Ferrat yet again? What about those times when you don't have enough time to *live* your life, much less *record* it?

Don't worry. You can keep your journal in under 15 minutes at a whack without ever feeling bored or boring. Here's how:

---

² Excerpted from *Journal to the Self: 22 Paths to Personal Growth,* © Kathleen Adams, New York: Warner Books, 1990.

1. **Keep a one-year diary.** They come in an attractive assortment of cover designs; many have matching scrapbooks and photo albums. Because the format restricts you to about 100 words, writing takes 10 minutes or less a day. And keeping your one-year diary on the nightstand by your bed has a sort of Victorian simplicity that is madly appealing.

2. **In the evening, write one adjective describing your day on your wall calendar.** Then, underneath it, write one adjective describing how you want tomorrow to be. This takes about one minute and becomes a fascinating exercise in creating your own reality.

3. **Best Thing/Worst Thing Springboards are great.** Repeated use of these Springboards will give you a running commentary on the highlights and blackouts of your life.

4. **Pick a theme word for a week or a month.** Choose a juicy word like happiness, loneliness, confusion, clarity, anger, passion or change. Spend 5-15 minutes each time writing about how you experienced the theme word.

5. **Find a moment from your day to capture in poetry or prose.** The rainbow out your office window, the elation when the home team won the game, the luxury of a bubble bath. If you can't find a moment to record, slow down a little. And start expecting miracles. They might just show up.

6. **Set the kitchen timer for 15 minutes.** Quit writing when it dings.

7. **Write a description of a stranger** — the person across from you on the train, the little blond kid in the bright red dress, someone you'll never see again, someone you haven't met yet.

8. **Jot down the one-liners** of philosophy, absurdity or spiritual revelation that wander through your mind. Hugh Prather's *Notes to Myself* is a (best-selling!) collection of just such "random" thoughts.

9. **Write a list of "10 Things I Want Off My List By Tomorrow."** Keep this list with you throughout the day and cross off items as you finish them.

10. **Write a Win List of anything at all that went right during the day.** (Yes, there are days when "getting out of bed" counts.) If you are in recovery from any sort of addictive behavior, be sure to list your recovery *every single day* as a win. If you're not getting at least a dozen a day, look harder.

11. **Write your journal on 3x5 index cards.** File entries by subject or date in a recipe box.

12. **Write a postcard.** Send it to yourself. The ultimate travel tip for journalers on the go — write your daily log on the back of picture postcards!

13. **"Flow write" for 10 minutes.** Start anywhere, go where you please.

14. **Thumb through an old magazine until a picture "sings" to you.** Clip the picture and paste it in your journal. Write about it.

15. **Write a prayer.** Write a letter to God, your Higher Self, Jesus Christ, your guardian angel, your patron saint, your inner wisdom. Let these entities write a letter to you.

Nature loves balance, and so there will be plenty of languid times to even out the hectic spans. These quieter times are the moments when you will drink deeply from the journal well. But your time crunch doesn't mean you must sacrifice your journal, and your journal doesn't mean you must sacrifice your time. As it is with nature, there is balance where you seek it.

ALL MORNING, READING

All morning, reading,
I watched it snow
and the words piled up
in drifts at my feet
stiff and cold as winter seeds.
All morning, reading,
flakes, fat and lazy
as dandelion spores snowed
into yesterday's snow, and
under my chair, poems rattled
like bones, hissed and clicked
like winter grasses. All morning,
reading, one small ember glowed
in the cave of my belly
turning the spaces between
flakes into the white
patches between words,
melted my resistance
and became this poem.

Amy Christman

Poetry Prompt

Take some activity of your day or week that has
absorbed or preoccupied you. Start a poem with
"All morning…." or "All day…." or "All week….".
Set the timer for 15 minutes. See where it goes.

CHAPTER 6

Writing in the Dark: Exploring Dreams in the Journal

"Who's got a dream?" I asked.

The dozen dreamers on weekend retreat looked slowly around the circle. For a full minute the only sound was the cheerful popping and crackling of the fire. Thin February sunlight danced through the blinds and shimmered in abstract stripes across Steve's chest. Gradually a dozen gazes rested on him.

Steve cleared his throat. "I had a dream about bricks."

"Will you tell us the dream?" I asked. "Tell it in the present tense, as if it is happening to you right now."

"I dreamed I was standing in front of—-"

"I am standing in front of—-" I coached.

"—-I am standing in front of some bricks. There are lots of them. Two men tell me to buy the bricks. I buy them, but I don't know what I'll build. Either a house or a wall. Then I see some cleared ground and I know that's where I'll build. There were some other details, but they don't seem as important."

"What's your best guess about how this dream relates to your life today?" I asked.

Steve frowned in concentration. "I don't know if this is right, but.... my wife died almost four years ago. I wonder if this dream is telling me that I'm ready to come out from behind my wall and begin building a new life for myself — or doomed to stay isolated and lonely."

Why Dreamwork?

Every night when you go to sleep, you script and direct a movie starring yourself. You create the sets, design the costumes, order in the props. You play every character. Your own life dramas are acted out on the stage of your psyche. You are the only audience. Each performance is startling in its freshness and creativity.

"Dreams are like letters baked into pies," says Jungian analyst Clarissa Pinkola Estes. They are answers to questions we haven't yet thought to ask. Dreams are like carved ivory Chinese balls that contain increasingly tinier and more intricately carved balls within them.

Dreams offer us glimpses into the inner workings of our own minds and hearts. They lift the veil between the worlds and drop a drawbridge. When you approach them with reverence and curiosity, your dreams will reward you by offering a map of your psyche and soul.

Journal work and dream work are natural allies. Just about every program of dream study recommends capturing your dreams in writing. From there you can process your dreams using a wide variety of journal techniques and devices.

Dreamwork lets you practice your intuition. When you encounter a truth, there is an unmistakable sensation of knowing. Your skin may tingle, you may gasp sharply, a cartoon light bulb might explode above you, you may feel zapped with a rush of energy. Dreamwork expert Jeremy Taylor calls this sensation the "aha of recognition" and attributes it to memory. Taylor writes:

> When you discover some true thing about a dream, you are likely to experience the aha of recognition because in that moment, you remember, consciously for the first time, what you already knew unconsciously the dream meant at the time it occurred.... The aha of recognition.... is the only reliable touchstone of dream work.[3]

Befriending Your Dreamkeeper

Dreams love to be noticed. The good news about this is that even if you don't remember your dreams now, you'll probably start remembering them once you pledge your attention to them.

Pay attention to dreams the same way you pay attention to friends knocking at your door: Invite them in. Ask them about themselves, and listen with interest when they answer. Offer your own ideas and opinions. Express appreciation for little gifts.

Invite your dreams to visit you by writing a note in your journal to the Dreamkeeper just before retiring. "Dear Dreamkeeper," you

---

[3] *Where People Fly and Water Runs Uphill*, Jeremy Taylor, New York: Warner Books, 1993.

might say. "Tonight I'd like a dream that I can remember and write down. I promise that I'll pay attention to it. Thanks!"

You can get as specific as you want in your request, asking for guidance and clarity about any number of life issues. Dreamkeepers are mighty obliging.

A week or so before I taught the dream journal workshop where Steve told his brick dream, I asked my Dreamkeeper for a dream that I could use as an opening story. That night I received a dream in which an old friend was pregnant. With her was her son, who in the dream was about seven years younger than he was in real life.

I awoke from this dream with a question: *What idea was I gestating about seven years ago that is now ready to be born?*

How was I going to make a story out of this dream? I didn't know.

Two nights before the workshop, I again asked my Dreamkeeper: "Tonight I request a dream that will help me turn the first dream into an opening story. Thanks. Over and out!" The next morning I awoke from a dream in which my father had a heart attack. There's a tendency to become alarmed when illness or death comes in a dream. But dreams containing scenes of accidents, heart attacks, sudden illnesses or even death aren't usually literal warnings. Like almost everything in the dream world, they are symbols and coded messages. So I gratefully accepted the *symbol* of my father's heart attack as an answer to my request. Now I had an exact date to work with — the date of my father's mild heart attack seven years earlier!

Within minutes I had uncovered the associations. When my father had his heart attack, I had just returned from teaching journal workshops in Arizona. At my Tucson workshop was a man who had recorded more than 5,000 dreams! He had three or four dreams a night and catalogued them meticulously. However, he had no idea how to interpret them. The class was so fascinated at his questions about dreams that I spontaneously added an extra session specifically on working with dreams in the journal. It was the first time I had formally taught ways to use the journal techniques I was teaching to crack the code of dreams.

So the question from my first dream, *What idea was I gestating about seven years ago that is now ready to be born?* was answered: Self-interpretation of dreams through journal writing. The story of how my Dreamkeeper obligingly led me down narrow cobblestone dream-streets to present me with my dream journal origins became the opening tale for my workshop.

Writing in the Dark

After you have invoked a dream, fall asleep with a sense of anticipation and receptivity. Then prepare yourself to record a dream, and plan some processing time into your day. Here are a baker's dozen suggestions for dream recall and journal work.

1. Record your dream upon awakening. Use the present tense to add immediacy and to honor the dream's ongoing life force. Don't remember the entire dream? Record scenes, fragments, snatches, even impressions. When it comes to dreamwork in your journal, a little can go a long way.

2. Name your dreams as you would a short story or painting or poem. Keep a separate, running list of your dream titles somewhere in your journal. Themes will often jump out at you.

3. If you don't remember your dreams, try writing a note to your "Dreamkeeper" in your journal before you turn out the lights. It might be as simple as, "Dear Dreamkeeper, Please bring me a dream that I'll remember tomorrow morning. I promise I'll write it down and pay attention to it. Thanks!"

4. After you've recorded your dream, write a Ten-Minute Sprint in which you give your best guess as to what this dream might be saying about your waking life.

5. Write a list of questions raised by the dream. Leave yourself a few lines between questions. Then go back and answer the questions. Do this quickly and without much conscious thought.

6. Cluster your dream symbols. When you get an "aha" of recognition, note it and use it as a symbol substitution for your dream.

7. Dialogue with your dream characters. Ask them why they're in your dream, what they're trying to communicate to you, how you can best understand their meaning.

8. Free write about a particularly elusive symbol or character. Let yourself free associate. Be alert for "ahas of recognition." (An "aha of recognition," according to dreamworker Jeremy Taylor, is the conscious mind remembering what the unconscious mind knew all along, but the conscious mind forgot.)

9. Write a Captured Moment of a scene from the dream, focusing on the sensory details. Extend this into a fictional scene. What if a character in a short story found her/himself in this very situation? What might happen next? Where might this action lead?

10. Shift perspectives. Take a key symbol or character from your dream and rewrite the dream as if that symbol or character were the dreamer. Or let the symbol/character interpret itself, by writing in the first person from its perspective ("I am the winding dirt road. I am in this dream because....").

11. Play Western Union. Rewrite the dream using as few words as possible, in telegram style. Let yourself be cryptic and direct. Often, nuances and layers of meaning will emerge.

12. Write a poem about the dream. Focus on the images and feelings. Try an AlphaPoem about a dream symbol, scene or character.

13. Draw, paint or sketch the dream or its symbols. Or make a collage using images that represent the dream. One woman in a recent workshop collaged a cover for her journal using her dream images and symbols. Her first entry in the journal helped her interpret the dream's meaning for her next steps.

DREAM

I wake to discover a shard
of last night's dream whirling
in the overhead fan, a single
image of rural America I've never
seen. Grain fields parted by long
straight roads, amber seas, the
rippled illusion of melting asphalt,
lemony sun in an acre of azure sky,
the angle of shadows at midday,
crows crouched at a remnant of puddle,
muttering, as if the brackish water
would refresh their tune, as if I won't
spend the day chasing words like
"penchant," and "hunker," as if this
road is a place I belong, a place
I remember, and not just the prick
and tease of last night's dream.

Amy Christman

Poetry Prompt

Record a dream that you have had recently, or that you
still remember from some time ago, as a poem.

FAMILIES AND RELATIONSHIPS

families Writing

A family journal is a cozy practice. Whether you write scrapbook-style, with each community member's offerings gathered in a three-ring notebook, or in a special blank book, you're creating precious family history. Here are eight ideas. The first two are adapted from Peter Stillman's excellent book *Families Writing*[4].

1. **Start a family newsletter.** Stillman tells the charming story of an 8-year-old in Illinois who wrote a hand-written newsletter, "The Family News," originally for distribution to her immediate family, but which quickly became renowned among extended family. Her mother reports that far-flung relatives and family friends communicate with this entrepreneurial journalist with considerably more frequency than anyone else in the family! Some typical entries from a June/July edition:

---

[4] *Families Writing, 2nd Ed.*, Peter Stillman, Portsmouth NH: Boynton & Cook, 1998.

Julie's Graduation. Julie graduated on June 13 from North Central College. Her degree is in Speech Communications and Theatre. Almost the whole family went to see her. Everybody cheered! The next day, Julie had her party. The whole family came! A disc jockey came! It was great!!
Matt News. Matthew has a new bed! He is out of the crib and in a twin bed that has a safty (sic) rail. When he gets up from his nap he goes over and knocks on the door and waits for Sue to come and get him! Matt grew 3 inches in 3 months! He loves riding in wagons!

2. **Gather up your stories.** According to Stillman, "(Family writing) has obvious and inestimable value in strengthening essential bonds." Consider a home-published collection of Captured Moments, poetry, and stories about one particular family member. One such booklet, *My Sister and I,* was written by an Idaho schoolteacher who created it for her sibling's 40th birthday. It contains moments and memories known only to the two of them — childhood adventures, pranks, secrets; sibling rivalries and jealousies; shared intimacies as adults. "Nothing extraordinary, heart-rending, grand," Stillman says. "Just the homely incidents of life, the unremarkable details, the common-place. Which is the raw material of all good writing and which is also why anyone, no matter how apparently uneventful his or her life, can't possibly ever run out of things to write about."

3. **Scribe your family legends.** My sister has created an intricate mythology for her children about the Tooth Fairy. Each child has her or his own assigned Tooth Fairy, with individual personalities, communication styles, and distinctive hand-writing. When I was a kid, my dad created an imaginary character, Yahootie, who always got blamed when one of us

wouldn't 'fess up: "So who ate the last of the ice cream? Yahootie?" Write stories about your family myths and legends — the ones you grew up with, the ones you create for your own children. Along the same line are stories about the most colorful characters in your family and their odd ways. My grandfather, an actual working cowboy in his youth, had a bawdy sense of humor and was legendary for his extensive collection of outhouse miniatures. When he died, we inventoried his entire stash before carting it off to Goodwill — a "list poem" that always brings down the house. This category of community writing would also include favorite holiday customs, traditions, stories and lore.

4. **Start a writing tradition.** One year for Christmas, a broke grandson offered his grandma a weekly letter from college — and then followed through. Their correspondence, and intimacy, continues. Start a tradition of tucking silly notes in lunch pails, love notes in pockets, goodnight notes under pillows. When I find an inspirational quote or message, I write it down, date it, and slip it into whatever book I'm currently reading. My original thought was to startle myself at some future point, but since many of those books have now found themselves in my lending resource library, I'm constantly being told by students and clients how the quote or thought prompted them into a writing session.

5. **Create a travelogue.** My best friend Marta is the consummate travel postcard writer. Her cards are funny and informative, with interesting, well-chosen photos. My collection of "Marta" postcards is an illustrated history of a 35-year friendship. One of my favorites came from a road trip through the Southwest. Her postcard showed a certain small town's Main Street, with

this note: *Dear Kay, I'm standing on a corner in Winslow, Arizona. I'm such a fine sight to see. There's a boy, my Lord, in a flatbed Ford, slowing down to take a look at me. Take it easy, Marta.* When you travel, even if it's only for the weekend, send a postcard to someone in the family.

6. **Circle the distance.** Far-flung families or communities can stay in touch with a circle journal or round-robin letter. *Caveat:* Put someone with strong organizational and follow-up skills in charge! During a women's writing retreat one summer, Shari suggested we circulate a "circle journal" to keep the connection. She mapped out the pathway, figured that it could make two complete circuits from Connecticut to Hawaii in about a year, if everyone kept it no longer than two weeks. We collectively created a collage for the journal cover during the last day of the retreat. Shari created easy-to-follow instructions, including the timeline and addresses, which she taped to the inside cover, and she made the first entry. Four months and ten months later, it circled around to me, and I delighted in both receiving and giving news.

7. **Storyboard your scrapbook.** As you gather photos and memorabilia for your albums or scrapbooks, jot one- or two-sentence captions. Occasionally devote a scrapbook page to a longer story. The streamlined version: Pester each family member to jot notes on the backs of fresh photos.

8. **Just the "write" gift.** Write a poem, a Character Sketch, a Captured Moment for a loved one. Typeset and illustrate it on the computer. Or write it out in your own hand on elegant or decorated paper. Frame it and give it as a gift.

PROUD FLESH

And see how the flesh grows back
across a wound, with a great vehemence,
More strong than the simple, untested surface before.
— *Jane Hirschfield, from* <u>For What Binds Us</u>

Even blind you could travel
the map of my undoing,
the raised flesh in patterns
like the sandy bottoms of
slow moving streams,
words left unspoken,
chances missed, useless
anger heaped under the skin,
worry, slick and pink as new
scars still warm to the touch.

And see how your hand seeks
those places, how you are
drawn to the thick ropes of
my wounds, how you play
them as if they were strings
meant for making music, and not
the soft shadows of old blows
that threatened to pull me under.

And see how your loving transforms,
how you lead me away from these
peaks and valleys, these striations
of lack and misdirection. See how

the damage becomes not simply the past
but the core around which I must grow,
and you are the grain of sand from which
I have grown this pearl I call my life.

Amy Christman

Poetry Prompt

Write a poem to someone in your family.
Into its container pour the tenderness, affection,
history and love that you share.

CHAPTER 8

Life Story Writing for Seniors

I was born on March 22, 1904 in Tecumseh, Oklahoma — Indian Territory. I am the youngest of ten children — five boys and then five girls. I had two very wise and wonderful parents. When I was 18 months old, my papa and mama each filed a claim on adjoining land farther up near the Panhandle of Oklahoma. We must have been traveling in covered wagons because we had an organ and all good things of Mama's. Mama was taking her side saddle. Later she cut off the leather flaps and half-soled us kids' shoes. She was a very efficient lady.

So begins the "memoirs" of Goggie, who, at age 86, began writing her life story at the urging of my sister, her granddaughter. Over the next several years, Goggie wrote or told dozens of vignettes that described homestead life in the Wild West — her father's accidental death, carving out a settlement in the midst of Indian country, her toys and playmates, holiday celebrations, the courtship and marriages of her siblings, her own marriage at the age of 17.

By the time Goggie reached her 90s, dementia had stolen her ability to write or even tell her own stories. Her daughters and grandchildren filled in the gaps, writing and telling those stories most familiar and beloved from their own experiences, and scribing Goggie's faltering reminiscences. When Goggie died at 95, her eulogy was crafted around the "memoirs" that had become a family heirloom. We fashioned the stories into a booklet, and this hand-made treasure will follow 13 great-grandchildren through the next generations.

One of the markers of a life well lived must surely be the stories, experiences and memories that are told, retold, remembered and re-experienced throughout the life span. Life story writing captures the priceless and the poignant, the truly memorable and the quirkily remembered, the historic and the unique. It leaves a legacy of living history for future generations. And it can bring enjoyment, satisfaction and closure in the last stage of life.

Of the many excellent books on autobiographical writing, perhaps the best for seniors is Lois Daniel's *How to Write Your Own Life Story*. Originally published in 1980, it came out of the author's sense that she had "completely failed" a 75-year-old student in a creative writing class:

> When I asked each student to state his or her reason for joining the class, this lady's reason was that for several years her children had been begging her to write the story of her life. "I don't know how to do it," she said, "and I thought you might be able to help me." Frankly, I had no idea how to help her.... I hadn't the faintest idea how to help a non-writer write the story of her life.[5]

---

[5] *How to Write Your Own Life Story*, 4th Ed., Lois Daniel, Chicago: Chicago Review Press, 1997.

Daniel suggests writing in small sketches, tiny vignettes of a few sentences. In addition to genealogical and family life stories — circumstances of birth, favorite toys, stories about siblings and grandparents — she suggests topics such as:

Where were you on important days in history?
Accomplishments of which you are the most proud
Children and the things they say
Inventions
Brief encounters

The thought of writing a life retrospective can daunt even the most experienced writer, so it is small wonder that it might feel too huge to even start. My sister originally engaged Goggie through correspondence, writing letters that asked a specific question. She included a piece of stationery and a self-addressed, stamped envelope, and most often received her answer within the week.

You asked me how we spent our Sunday afternoons. We went to community Pie Suppers, and we also had Box Suppers. The boxes were decorated with pretty paper and Mama made a handle on it with a big bow. We put lunches, doughnuts, cake or whatever we had — goodies in the bag and it was auctioned off to the highest bidder to raise money for something. I'll never forget how Jim Rodgers never failed to get my oldest sister's box. He always paid the most. The auctioneers would see to that.

Life story writing is an excellent way to build community with other seniors. Anne Flaxman, a certified instructor with the Center for Journal Therapy, teaches memoir writing for seniors in Fairfield County, Connecticut, as well as traveling around the country seeding new life story writing groups. Benefits of writing in a structured class include the guidance of a writing prompt, the coaching of a trained facilitator, the enjoyment of hearing the stories of others, and the power of writing and sharing one's own story to a listening audience. Writing in a group also decreases isolation, reawakens dormant interests, offers purposeful activity and hones cognitive skills.

"One of the most important thing that happens in a seniors memoir group," says Flaxman, "is the way these people begin to see their lives as jewels that have been polished through time and experience and living. They begin to see the beauty and uniqueness that their life has represented."

Flaxman's course, divided into 8 "chapters" or sessions, follows a chronological pathway through personal history. Seniors begin with "Before My Story Starts" (reflections on family history and ancestry) and end with "Before I Go" ("ethical wills" and other last words). The "ethical will" writing process begins with a list of 10 Things I Want My Loved Ones to Know — ethics, beliefs, mottos, other things seniors want others to know about what they have learned in their lifetimes. "From there," Flaxman said, "the ethical will evolves into a document that acknowledges and passes on the qualities, causes and values that an individual life has stood for. Lady Bird Johnson, for instance, might include in her ethical will the importance of natural beauty in everyday life, and the legacy of a more beautiful America."

Overall, Flaxman says, the seniors who pass through her classes learn to see themselves as part of a historical landscape that spans an entire century — and they are frequently awed at the way their individual lives have intersected and almost touched. "Three people in one class saw the Hindenberg on its last day," she said. "One saw it fly overhead, one saw smoke in the next field, and one's father was a doctor who was called to the scene."

Sometimes fragile bones or faltering senses make physical writing difficult or impossible. Family members or support persons can assist by scribing "spoken poems." To maintain authentic voice, preserve language exactly as it is heard, including phonetic spellings and idiosyncratic grammar. One of Goggie's spoken stories makes a charming poem simply by adding line breaks:

> *I played by myself a lot.*
> *Up in the orchard, playing with the frogs and the birds.*
> *One time I got too close to a scissor-tail bird's nest in the orchard*
> *and it swept down and touched my hair on top.*
> *Maybe you think I didn't scram from the orchard*
> *hollering "Mama! Mama!"*
> *Once I caught a big frog and a little frog*
> *and I tied the little frog to its mother's back*
> *so it wouldn't have to walk.*
> *I learned to whistle up in the orchard.*

Family members can be encouraged to contribute their own memories for additional perspective. Goggie's daughter writes:

> *She made all our clothes. We can't remember ever having seen a store-bought pattern in the house, but we do remember fidgeting impatiently while she begged us to stand still long enough for her to take our measurements. Then she would lay newspaper out on the table and cut out the patterns for our puffed sleeve, full-skirted dresses.*

The compiling and "publishing" of the stories can be done by a computer-literate grandchild or great-grandchild as a limited edition for the family. I was privileged to speak her eulogy, compiled of stories chronicled over the years, and now we continue the stories for another generation:

> *I did not fully see the beauty in my grandmother's life until I delivered her eulogy. I did not see the enormous tapestry of*

creative threads. All manner of craft. Nothing left out —
sewing, fabric art, macramé, pillow tufting, embroidery, rug
hooking, crocheting, knitting, jewelry-making, singing,
recording, painting, sculpting, woodworking, rock polishing,
gardening, dancing. She did it all, with the possible exception
of writing, and she did that at the end. This original voice, this
pioneer woman educated for nine years in a one-room
schoolhouse lived a brilliantly creative life. What an honor it is
to be her grandchild.

Writing Your Life Story: Six Suggestions for Seniors

1. Write in small sketches of 5-10 minutes on specific topics, such as a favorite holiday, the first job, a memorable world event.

2. Engage family members in the process. Invite correspondence, or ask nearby relatives to scribe "spoken poems" by writing down everything that is said, in your exact words.

3. Join a life story or memoir writing group. Ask at your senior center, library, or doctor's office. If a writing group doesn't exist, see if you can get one started.

4. Tell the stories of how you participated in world history. Where were you when you heard about the bombing of Pearl Harbor? How did you and your family spend the Great Depression years? Where were you when President Kennedy was assassinated?

5. Write your "ethical will." What life learnings, personal philosophies, mottos, and core values do you want to leave as legacy to your descendants? How did you learn these lessons or acquire these philosophies?

6. Ask someone in your family with computer skills to compile your stories into a self-published memoir. Scan in family photos and memorabilia for illustration.

After Theodore Roethke's "I remember how it was to drive in gravel"

Hours on the road, and strip malls
melted into the wrinkled laps
of sagging barns, into the metallic
ping of oiled gravel. I remember
the mud-slick road, baked hard
as concrete, studded with rocks
that appeared suddenly, like teeth,
the open mouth of a hungry snake.
On the road North of Peterborough
bright tunnel of green, trees and brush
approaching like wary dogs, sniffing
as we passed, closing quietly behind,
we never knew how completely
we were being devoured, our own
hunger louder and more insistent.
Somewhere on that road, a part of me
sat up and paid attention, to the scent
of pine and leaf mold, low mounds
of hills reflected in the soft sherbet
mirror of a still lake, to fish caught
and eaten, within an hour, wild
raspberries, sun-warm and tart
in sweet cold milk, the way rain
pools in the waxy folds of leaves.
I remember how it felt to be aware,
for the first time, of how I fit

inside my body, how it felt to be
small in a large space, the shape
the feel, the taste of true wilderness.

Amy Christman

Poetry Prompt

Interview an elder family member, or jot down
reminiscences you recall from family stories or your
own childhood experiences with a grandparent or
senior. Craft them into a poem.

CHAPTER 9

Love Letters

Who among us doesn't love a love letter? Here are 31 suggestions — one for each day of the month — to help you explore the many dimensions of your appreciation and care. Write one every day. Start on the 1st of the month, or start with whichever number represents today's date and keep going until you've completed the full cycle.

Letters are one of the three primarily relational journal techniques (Dialogue and Character Sketch are the others) and are intentionally designed to be a one-way communication. Since you have the entire stage, you can feel free to express yourself in as much detail, and with as much emotion, as you wish. However, before you send your letter, tuck it away overnight. Perhaps stash it beneath your pillow, to literally sleep on it. Read it again the following day. If it feels right, mail it. If not, leave it in your journal. There's plenty of benefit from just having written the letter.

Devote yourself to a full month of open-heartedness. Notice what happens to the quality of your relationships, personal empowerment, and energy.

1.   Who is your dearest friend? Write a letter telling her/him what you value, appreciate and enjoy about your friendship. Share a favorite moment.

2.   Write a letter to someone in your local community whose leadership or volunteer work you admire.

3.   What's your favorite restaurant? What do you love about it? Drop the owner, manager or a special waitperson a note.

4.   Write your employer or supervisor a note of appreciation for your job. If you're self-employed, write to yourself.

5.   Bodyworker Anne Rojo says, "Why not fall in love with the body you've been sleeping with every night of your life?" Write a love letter to your body.

6.   As an author, I deeply appreciate letters from readers who have enjoyed my books. Write to a favorite author today. If you can't find an address in the book or on the Internet, send it in care of the publisher — it may take a while, but it will be forwarded.

7.   Write a love letter to someone in your family or extended family who is older than you.

8.   What is your special creative talent or gift? Write a love letter to your Muse, expressing thanks for inspiration to express your creativity.

9. Write a love letter to someone who makes you laugh.

10. Write a love letter to your best friend from high school or college.

11. What teacher from your childhood or adolescence really made a positive difference in your life? Write a letter to him or her. This is a good one to send, if the teacher can be found.

12. Write a love letter to a friend from the animal kingdom — a current or former pet, the birds at the feeder, a member of an endangered species.

13. Write an e-mail of appreciation or admiration to someone you know, or know of, only from the Internet.

14. Write a love letter to the love of your life — past, present or future.

15. What is the place you call home? Write a love letter to your physical dwelling, neighborhood, city, state or region.

16. Entire ancient civilizations worshipped the sun, knowing that no earthly life could be sustained without it. Write a love letter to the sun, or to your favorite natural element.

17. Write a love letter to someone in your family or extended family who is younger than you.

18. Write a letter of gratitude and appreciation to someone who helps care for your body — physician, massage therapist, dental hygienist, pharmacist.

19. Write a love letter to someone who has been like a father to you.

20. We all have habits or behavior patterns that we'd like to change. Today, choose one, and instead of cursing it, write a love letter to it.

21. Write a love letter to someone who serves you in the course of everyday life — the grocery check-out clerk, your mail carrier, your auto mechanic, your financial advisor.

22. Write a letter of appreciation to a political figure whose leadership you admire and support.

23. Write a love letter to someone who has been like a mother to you.

24. Write a love letter to a beautiful place in nature where you go to be restored.

25. Write a letter to a charity or nonprofit organization that puts love into action. Enclose a check.

26. Write a love letter to your guardian angel, spirit guide, patron saint, Higher Self, clergy, or other spiritual wisdom figure.

27. Write a love letter to whatever or whoever once saved your life, literally or metaphorically.

28. Write a love letter to your Emerging Self — the "you" you are becoming.

29. Write a note of support and well-being to a person less fortunate than you. Wrap a dollar bill around it and hand it to the next person you see who is asking for help.

30. Write a love letter to the person you were as a child or adolescent.

31. Write a love letter to God.

THIS LOVE CAN FLY

This love began
airy as the bones of small birds,
dry and light as dropped seeds,
its weight barely enough to keep
it earthbound. We each hold
tightly to a feather's empty shaft,
learn to steal the lift and power
from those qualities we honor
in each other. We listen to
the rich pulse of rapid breathing,
watch missteps and wrong
words curl into slick balls of
standing water, beads of apology
and forgiveness we roll in our
fingers, releasing vital oils scented
with promise. We throw wide our
arms and release expectation
because this love can fly.

Amy Christman

Poetry Prompt

Choose someone or something in your life that you love.
Go through magazines and cut out words and phrases that
resonate with you as you hold the beloved in your mind.
Arrange the words and phrases on a piece of colored
stationery or construction paper. Move them around until
you have a poem. Glue them down. Voila! A poetry collage.

ILLNESS, TRAUMA AND RECOVERY

CHAPTER 10

And All Is Well: Jihan's Story

I.

My first hint that something was seriously wrong came on a Post-It note.

"I wrote these after writing group," Jihan scribbled. "Thoughts?"

"These" were about 20 short AlphaPoems, typed neatly in two columns over three pages, all using the word BREAST as an organizing theme. Individually, they were small jewels of expression. Collectively, they told a troubled story of a woman deeply concerned.

Jihan Matteson, 57, had been an active member of my Monday afternoon journal therapy group for over a year when she wrote these poems one January. Already a survivor of breast cancer, she had used the writing group to map out the unfamiliar terrain of life after recovery. What she kept hearing in her writing was the maddening instruction to sit still. And in the stillness, increasingly, she received messages that all was not well with her breast.

As the poems and writings bubbled up from a place deep within, Jihan sought opinions and answers. She began with her colleagues and friends at the healing arts center where she worked as an administrator. Before long, Jihan had grim news: Her cancer was back, virulent and nasty. As referral led to referral, she landed at Denver's University Hospital with a leading research oncologist, who diagnosed her with Stage 4+ breast cancer, metastasized to the liver.

Where does one turn, but to family, friends and faith? Jihan wrote an e-mail to her dearest childhood friend, Mary. Mary wrote back. Jihan wrote again, this time copying her daughter and son. Mary's daily e-mails of support and strength became a lifeline for her. Exhausting as it was to try and keep her far-flung family apprised of her constantly changing medical situation, Jihan added more names to the "cc" field of her e-mail. She forwarded me one of her missives one day. "It sounds like you're writing an e-mail journal," I said. "Can I be on the list?" The Monday afternoon writing group clamored for inclusion. So did others in her extended family. Before long, there were 30 who received daily updates on her treatment, as well as a window into her moods, thoughts, emotions, needs and daily life.

We shared in Jihan's deepest internal discourse about the meaning of life and the reality of death. We were treated to delightful portraits of her baby granddaughter, Bella, as she grew from infancy to toddlerhood. As silent witnesses, we suffered the agony and devastation of chemotherapy and its aftermath. Nearly every day, sometimes more than once, we received e-mails chronicling Jihan's struggle, strength and indomitable spirit. She was fond of quoting the medieval saint Julian of Norwich, and often ended her e-mails, "And all is well, and all is well, and all manner of things are exceedingly well."

In addition to chemotherapy, Jihan received weekly treatments of Healing Touch and Reiki, two energetic healing modalities. Each time she received a treatment, she wrote an e-mail journal entry about it, describing not only her own internal response but also the practitioner's insights, instructions and procedures. As a journal therapist, I was elated to read this dual perspective, as I know that writing in detail about a healing experience does wonders to anchor it into the body at a cellular level. Jihan's capacity to integrate and synthesize her healing experiences in writing, offered to an audience of concerned and compassionate others who were willing to simply witness and receive without judgment or argument, played a pivotal role in her healing process.

In August, after she finished her first round of chemotherapy, and after eight months of weekly Healing Touch and Reiki treatments, and after hundreds of e-mail journal entries, Jihan's CAT scans showed .... no trace of cancer in her liver or her breast. Her oncologist was frankly amazed. So, for that matter, were the rest of us, although we gladly embraced the opportunity to adjust to good news.

The treatments, and the healing, continued throughout the rest of the year. She began a second, much less disruptive, chemotherapy protocol. Her weekly Healing Touch and Reiki sessions continued, as did her near-daily e-mail journal entries. Her family and friends still offered abiding love and support. Her laughter came back, along with her hair. Her granddaughter Bella celebrated her first birthday, mastered walking, and began speaking English. Jihan completed the year in a state of deep gratitude and peace. And standing as permanent testament and chronicle of an extraordinary year was a manuscript-length journal of grace and grit, surrender and serenity, courage and challenge, healing and humor. And all was well, and all was well, and all manner of things were exceedingly well.

II.

Several weeks later, in February, Jihan and I had a conversation behind a closed door. She was beginning to feel the stirrings of internal disruption. Although her tests continued to show no progression of disease, the voice of her intuition, as it revealed itself through writing, was cause for concern.

"If I die," she said, "I want you to be my literary trustee. Take custody of all my cancer journals, and see if you can edit them into a book."

A few weeks later, tests revealed many small tumors in her brain. A series of high-intensity radiation treatments followed. As her strength and energy dwindled, so did her journal entries.

III.

Jihan entered Hospice of St. John in June, after her doctor told her she had 4-6 months to live. She visited three hospices and chose St. John's because it had a chapel, a cocktail hour and a chocolate cart.

IV.

My annual women's writing retreat at Benet Pines, a retreat center tucked away in a remote forested area in south central Colorado, began on Tuesday, June 19. On Monday, I stopped by St. John's on my way out of town. Jihan lay flat in bed, bald, beautiful, brilliant with radiance. She joked with me and told me to come back the next week and tell her all about "summer camp."

I returned home on Sunday evening. The next day, June 25, I received a call from Jihan's daughter. "They've just put Mom on watch," she said. "Can you come right away?"

I could, and did. As I held Jihan's hand, I read to her the prayers and notes written for her by women at "summer camp" and sang her a song about Julian of Norwich that a retreat participant had taught us:

> Ring on, bells of Norwich, and let the winter come and go,
> And all will be well again, I know.
> All will be well, I'm telling you, let the winter come and go
> And all will be well again, I know.

Jihan died that evening.

GATHERING TIMES

This is the season
of thaw and freeze,
of dearth and plenty.
These are the gathering times.
This landscape lies
wrapped in the detritus
of seasons past,
pods and casings,
bits of feather and bone,
skins tried on and discarded.

This is the season
of ask and reach,
of need and wanting.
These are the gathering times.
I will give you a map
of these hills and hollows,
this river that runs through me, humming.
Walk these curves
of hip and thigh, this belly
laid bare by winter winds.
Snow has gathered in tattered drifts
between my breasts.

This is the season
of clutch and grab
of cradle and hold.
Let your arms become a bower
of sunlight, I will hold your warmth.

Give me the fire of your earth,
the heat of your breath
on the frozen fields of my hunger.
Thaw me, fill me,
these are the gathering times.

Amy Christman

Poetry Prompt

Jihan's long season of dying was, by her own
description, among the most vital and vibrant times
of her life span, when she was a voracious
gatherer of experiences. Write a poem that
begins with "These are the _____ times"
or "This is the season of...."

CHAPTER 11

Diary of a Headache

Session One

Margo came to see me because her head hurt.

"I've tried everything!" she told me. A health professional married to another in her field, Margo had access to the finest treatment in town, both traditional and alternative, for her debilitating headaches. "I've tried acupuncture, biofeedback, chiropractic. I've tried medication, meditation, relaxation, guided imagery. Yoga. Prayer. Nutrition. Neurologists. I've got my headaches medically managed as well as they can be, but I know there's another level that I haven't addressed. That's what I want your help with."

Had she tried writing? "I write in a journal, but I don't think I'm doing it right. I'm not getting results. Mostly I just write about the day — what I did, who I saw, what's on for tomorrow. I think I should be writing about my feelings, but I don't know how to do that. And I'm so tired all the time that I can barely hold my pen as it is."

I could sense the pain behind Margo's eyes. I thought about the worst headache I ever had and imagined it coming on suddenly and often. "How long do you spend on your daily entries?"

"I don't know, ten or fifteen minutes, maybe. I try to write before I go to bed, three or four times a week."

"That's good," I said. "That's probably enough. I don't think you'll need to do much more than what you've already scheduled. Now, tell me about your headaches. I know you are an expert on them. Tell me how often they come, what brings them on, what helps relieve them."

Margo and I spent the rest of our first session gathering information. She was, as I expected, an expert on her own problem. I assigned homework: Create a chronological health history, with special focus on headaches. I suggested she use continuous-feed computer paper to make a horizontal time chart from birth to the present time in which she was to note incidences of illness, injury, chronic pain or other health difficulty, as well as healing activities such as new treatments, medications, natural healings or other health improvements. It would be helpful, I said, if she'd also include major life transitions and events that had a decidedly emotional feel to them.

I also invited her to continue her evening writes, with one simple shift: Move her focus to the interior life. I gave her a list of "writing from within" journal questions and prompts.

> *How do I feel right now? Emotionally? Physically?*
> *Mentally? Spiritually?*
> *My heart wants to say—-*
> *Today I was aware of—-*
> *What wants to be known?*
> *The name of this feeling is ——*

"Choose one of these topics, and write for ten or fifteen minutes, just like you've been doing," I said. "Follow the thread of your writing wherever it leads you. Don't try to figure out where it's going. Just let yourself write."

Session Two

Margo brought in her health history, all seven feet of it, with color-coded entries for problems, solutions and major life events. Her headaches and remedies were additionally highlighted in yellow. We draped it over my office chairs and admired it from a distance before fan-folding it into the headache years.

Margo anticipated my first question. "What I notice about this is that my headaches seemed to start at about the same time my family was undergoing quite a few events." We talked about her husband's acceptance of a new hospital position, her daughter's transition into adolescence, her son's emerging complexity. None of this was inherently negative or problematic, but neither was it easy.

"Another thing I notice," she said, "is that I'm building up a powerful resentment of these headaches. I noticed these in my evening writes. I'm really angry at them for disrupting my life so dramatically. I think of them as the Enemy."

"Would you be willing to explore this resentment using guided imagery and inner work?" I asked. Margo nodded. "Then close your eyes and take a couple of deep breaths. Now, allow an image of your headache to come to you. This image might come in any number of ways, so just take the first image you receive. Tell me when you've got it."

"It's.... it's a dark cloud," Margo said. "My headaches are a dark, dense, heavy storm cloud."

Margo's homework for the second session: Return to the storm cloud in imagery, and invite it to "talk" with her in the journal. I coached her on the Dialogue technique, a written conversation where she would write in two voices — her own, and the voice of the storm cloud. This sounded like an odd and difficult task, but she agreed to try. I also encouraged her to keep up her inner-focused evening writes.

Session Three

Margo arrived in the aftermath of a headache. A moderate one had plagued her for two full days. "Fortunately I'd done the Dialogue earlier in the week, because I never would have been able to focus on it during the headache," she said. "And it was easier than I expected, just like you said. In fact, I was amazed at how easily it flowed once I got started."

Me: *You still appear to me as a big, dark, heavy cloud but I see your face now and it is kind. I don't think you want to be a disturbance, but that is how I feel about you.*

HA: I'm ready to talk to you — I won't come into your head while we talk. I usually wait to be invited into your head.

Me: *I don't think I consciously invite you. Why do you come? What are you trying to tell me? My life is so comfortable and I am so blessed — you are an annoyance and a disturbance that I need to deal with and get rid of.*

HA: You like things to be "just so" and avoid conflict and disturbance but I think you need those things in your life, too.... Maybe you don't do the inviting consciously, but I do come by invitation.

"What is most interesting to you about this Dialogue?" I asked.

"Two things," Margo said. "First, that a pretty bad headache came on just after I finished it. I can't help but think of that as punishment. And second, when I was lying down waiting for my medication to take effect I brought up the image of the storm cloud and twice I thought I saw a face."

We went right into a guided imagery in which I invited her to let the clouds dissipate enough to see the face behind them. Margo opened her eyes, which were filled with amusement. "It's Yoda!" she said. "You know — from Star Wars?"

"Get your notebook," I said. "Write everything you know about Yoda. Five minutes, starting now. Ready, set, GO!"

We spent the rest of the hour probing the symbol of Yoda — a gentle, wise, ancient teacher — as spokesperson for her headaches. Margo's homework: A journal dialogue with Yoda, in which she was to ask how her headaches were her teacher.

Session four

Margo reported one small headache easily managed with medication. We turned to her dialogue with Yoda.

> Me: *I've not experienced a headache for over a week and I'm almost scared to say so for fear I'll now get one. Maybe talking with you helps me avoid dealing with you as a painful intrusion.*
>
> HA: I'm here to help you.
>
> Me: *Is there a connection between you and my inability to recognize and deal with anger? Are we on the right track?*

HA: This is one of the tracks. Holding in emotions is just who you are — you were taught to be quiet and humble and not draw attention to yourself. Although you've come a long way, you still feel guilty or embarrassed when you "let go."

Me: *Trying to remember events and emotions from the past is very uncomfortable. I feel very uncomfortable and anxious.*

HA: Look into your heart, express your emotions, and learn.

What had she learned from this process? "I'm amazed at the idea that my headaches are trying to be helpful," she said. "It never occurred to me that they might have a positive function."

We turned our focus to the suppressed feelings that manifested as headaches. Margo described a lifetime history of avoiding anger. The only child of peaceloving parents, she grew up with nonviolence as a primary ethic, and conflict was always managed with reason. While she was genuinely grateful for this orientation to healthy problem-solving, she was aware of just how little it had prepared her to live in a household where people sometimes got mad and yelled at each other.

In fact, Margo was beginning to realize how little she actually knew about the emotion of anger. What did normal, healthy anger look and feel like? When was it out of control? How could she not take it personally when someone in her family got mad? How could she begin to safely express anger herself?

"When was the last time you remember experiencing anger?" I asked. Margo concentrated. "I honestly don't remember.....Oh! Wait!" She paged rapidly through her journal. "Here it is — a couple of weeks ago, when I was first writing about feelings, and I realized how resentful and mad I was at my headaches."

"So anger is a feeling you recognize and experience," I said.

Margo gazed at me. "Yes," she slowly agreed. "But as I think about it now, I'm realizing that the only time I feel anger is when it's directed at myself."

The Next Sessions

I saw Margo three more times over the next two months. She continued to learn about anger, and how to direct it where it belongs, instead of automatically turning it inward. "Yoda" became a frequent journal companion, the voice of wisdom and healing within her. A journal log of her headache patterns revealed that they continued to come less frequently, with less intensity, and with better pain control through medication.

Fifteen Minutes to Wellness

If you, like Margo, have chronic pain or persistent difficulty of any sort, try writing your way to wellness. Here are six ideas. Unless otherwise indicated, take about 15 minutes for each write.

1.   **Make a list of everything you know about your pain,** illness, injury or difficulty. Be as specific and detail-oriented as you can. Include everything. If you think it, ink it. Keep your pen moving and sprint through a 15-minute write.

2.   **Make a health history time chart.** You can start from birth, or you can begin with the onset of the illness or difficulty. This will likely take about 30 minutes to set up; from there, you can add to it in 15-minute increments.

3. **Write from within.** Use interior-focused questions and prompts to focus yourself, then follow the pen. Stop at the end of 15 minutes. Re-read what you've written, and continue if you wish.

4. **Ask for an image of your pain,** illness or condition. Dialogue with the image you receive. (Dialogues take longer — schedule 30-45 minutes.)

5. **Every three or four entries, re-read your journal** and give yourself feedback. Write, "As I read this, I notice—."

6. **Keep a pain or symptom log** to document decreases in intensity, frequency, down time, and other variables specific to your own illness or concern.

THE HEADACHE GONE

Bright swirl of pain
precedes the freefall into
restless dreams touched
with swirls of color and hollow-
eyed strangers whispering
behind green walls of dripping
ivy. Time changes when you
sleep, visions howl and dance
lasting well into waking and
daylight, pride flutters like
a cast-off dress, your nakedness
not unbecoming, your need
released in a howl of desperation,
thick yellow ring of heat like
a tightly closed fist opening
towards soft gold, the absence
of pain a quiet thrum of relief.

Amy Christman

Poetry Prompt

Consider a chronic illness or pain, or remember a time
when you were sick or hurting. Find the place in your
body that holds this pain. Breathe deeply into that place,
and allow the stories of your pain and your healing to
pour through your fingers onto the page.

CHAPTER 12

Making Up the Truth

The Dark Men in my dreams would populate a psychopathic colony.
There are hundreds of them, varying only in the degree of their
malevolence. They all have one intent — to harm me — and they are
endlessly creative. They are torturers, terrorists, hijackers, kidnappers,
rapists, pirates and thieves. They are muggers, marauders, murderers,
outlaws, gangsters, con artists and crooks. They threaten. They menace.
They stalk. Whether they travel alone or in packs, they tear out my
phone lines, unlock my deadbolts, power through my barriers, kick
down my doors and paralyze my nerve endings.

—from <u>The Dark Man and Other Dreams,</u>
a short story by Kathleen Adams, ©1997

Once upon a time, in another decade, I loved a man who lied.
Although our lives intersected in the most charming of ways
— he wrote me a letter when my first book, *Journal to the Self,* was
published — and although our friendship unfolded slowly, stuffed in

hundreds of envelopes over seasons and years, still he deceived me through a web of intricately plotted and increasingly complex lies.

Deena Metzger says in *Writing for Your Life*[6], "To write is, above all else, to construct a self." This man constructed a self that had no foundation in three-dimensional reality. He created himself as fictional character, protagonist in a parallel universe, star of the life he should have had.

Meanwhile, my three-dimensional reality seemingly had no relationship to my self. I was struggling with a reality warp of my own. In a complicated inverse, my life was feeling like a novel. Everything I had ever dreamed of was happening to me, including a well-hailed first book and a brilliant, charming penfriend who was beginning to hint that I might be the woman he had been waiting for all his life.

Is this a story, or what? Romance, passion, paradox; destiny; weavings and layerings and inevitabilities. One waits a lifetime for such a story. I happily tumbled headfirst into love, and stayed there for a while.

You can discern the rest: It ended badly. The Glamour failed one day, and he was revealed as who he really was, or at least exposed as who he wasn't. Thus began a waking nightmare that lasted for most of the next year.

I have a shelf full of journals from that year. I wrote vociferously about my horror, rage, shock, self-recrimination, devastation, grief. For three seasons, my journal was a lifeline. It held my days together,

---

[6] *Writing for Your Life*, Deena Metzger, San Francisco: HarperSanFrancisco, 1992.

giving me cause both to get out of bed in the morning and into bed at night.

Woody Allen once said, "After 25 years of psychoanalysis, I have a brilliant understanding of my neurosis." After three seasons, I had a brilliant understanding all of the ways in which my journal was sounding more and more like an endless loop tape. I had processed all I could possibly process. I understood what I could, and the rest was incomprehensible.

I began to sense that there was something else that needed and wanted to happen. As odd as it may sound, the story became its own living, breathing thing. It was a palpable presence, this story – this story that was not treatise nor analysis nor catharsis nor endless "now" moment, but instead was mythic, archetypal, terribly real fiction. It lived in the dreamworld, the place that Dana Reynolds calls "sacred imagination." Through the mythic ages it has been told and enacted as the story of Psyche and Eros, or the story of Persephone's descent into the Underworld, or the story of Rapunzel in her tower, or Inanna's nine gates of hell, or the Dark Man. Especially the Dark Man.

The Dark Man is one of the 17 most prominent archetypes in women's dreams, according to Jungian analyst Clarissa Pinkola Estes. Nearly every woman I know has woken up from nightmares in which she experienced the terror and helplessness of being chased, raped or trapped by a thug, monster, ex, con artist or other devilish shapeshifter. Sometimes these dreams hold the psyche's imprint of trauma, or our own individual or collective shadow. Clarissa says they represent a creative part of the dreamer's psyche that is screaming to get out. Whatever it meant, I was living in the middle of a Dark Man dream, and as story, it begged to be written.

I had no idea how to write a short story, but my friend Paula was signed up for a writing class with short story master Pam Houston, so I signed up with her. Over the next four months I produced three torturous, arduous and ultimately thrilling drafts of a 30-page short story, *The Dark Man and Other Dreams,* that told the story of a woman, a man, and deception.

In the course of the writing, I underwent a tremendous transformation. The creative process being what it is, of course, I will never truly know what happened, but I know that something deep within me became healed as I immersed myself in the story, and the writing of the story. As I made up the truth, the truth set me free.

What made the difference? Mastery, craft, poetic truth and surrender.

Mastery. The first thing I noticed was that as omniscient narrator, I had all the information — something I completely lacked in the relationship. The power of mastery over how the story was told, what was revealed and what withheld, was utterly exhilarating. For years I had lived in a cloud of unknowing. Suddenly I knew everything. It was a radically powerful experience.

Craft. Next I found that the crafting of good sentences, the exquisite labor of breathing in and breathing out, the devotional stepping into language, the mindfulness of syllable and rhythm, became a transcendent experience, fashioning art out of horror. I took one of my life's most negative experiences and crafted it into one of my life's best pieces of writing.

Poetic truth. The decision to write fiction freed me from my fundamental journal ethic to tell the truth. Because it was fiction, I could write anything at all. I could create myself and my experience in the image of a character with a name (Julianna) and a sister (Rosie) and a Dark Man (Joseph) all her own. Through becoming absorbed in Julianna's reality, which was similar to my own but not the same as historical truth, I came to poetic truth.

Surrender. Lastly, I surrendered to the undertow of the Story that wove its way into every strand of words. Through mastery, craft and poetic truth, I was scribing my own individualized imprint of mythology. In my one small life, I was healing myself from a painful break-up. In the vast theatre of the sacred imagination, I was playing Psyche, or Persephone, or Rapunzel, or Inanna to a sell-out crowd.

Making up the truth healed me. Perhaps it can heal you, too. If you want to try this, here's a five-step process that I use with my writing groups, adapted from a method I learned from Deena Metzger.

1. Take a situation or circumstance in your life that troubles you. It can be a devastating event, or a chronic condition or problem. Write about it for 15 minutes. Then boil your 15-minute write into a one-sentence declaration of the situation.

2. Create a character who has many of the same strengths, qualities, characteristics, challenges and desires as you do, but who is not necessarily hobbled by your restrictions, limitations or obstacles. Write a Character Sketch of this character.

3. Set a scene. Get a picture in your mind of your character and the situation. Have your character begin taking some sort of action. Write a description.

4. From there, follow your character. Let yourself be guided. It is normal to not know what you're going to write next. Just let it happen.

5. Don't worry too much about writing in chronological order. In my writing groups, we write "pieces" or "squares" and then quilt them together later on.

MAKE USE OF SUFFERING

Make use of suffering
the way a dogwood makes use of
wind, its life spread out on updrafts
and currents of air, dropping with
grace and a flutter into bright pools
of rich earth to be born again.

Make use of suffering
the way forests are built
by swallows and chickadees
absently scattering seeds
that cling to feathers and
drop from too-full beaks.

Make use of suffering
the way bees kiss pollen
from tongue to tongue
making honey in tight cells.

Work provides its own lessons,
balm extracted from thorny thistles
opens into vibrant delicate flowers.
Become the seed and the carrier,
sticky with possibility. Choose
to either bury or nurture the
suffering that forms the chrysalis
from which you must finally emerge.

Amy Christman

Take one of your own experiences of suffering.
How has it molded and shaped you? Are there ways in
which you are better, stronger, wiser because of the
experience? Try a poem in which every stanza
begins with, "I make use of suffering….."

CHAPTER 13

Managing Grief through Journal Writing

A poet can take all the grief from her heart
(the pain that can swell and break a heart)
and write it in fine black lines
on starchy white paper. . . .
          —*from <u>Fine Black Lines</u>,* Lois Tschetter Hjelmstad[7]

I'm sick of it! I'm sick of sadness and pain. And I hate this
journal for pointing it out to me <u>all the time</u>. I hate you, journal!
          —*from the grief journal of Rachel,*
               as told in <u>Journal to the Self,</u> Kathleen Adams

Conventional wisdom tells us that writing a journal in times of catastrophic trauma is a good and helpful thing to do. The "fine black lines/ on starchy white paper" are kind and patient. They

---

[7] *Fine Black Lines,* Lois Tschetter Hjelmstad, OH: R&B Publications, 1993.

witness without judgment, contain without confinement, fill up and become more in the process of catharsis. As a psychotherapist who has specialized for nearly 20 years in the power of writing to heal body, psyche and soul, I know this to be true.

Imagine my surprise to learn, many years ago, that two-thirds of my clients who experienced traumatic stress, such as the death of a loved one, related to Rachel, above! They described writing in a journal as difficult, frightening, overwhelming or counterproductive.

This seeming paradox gave me pause, and I immediately set out to learn two things: Why is this so? And what can be done about it?

This is what I discovered: Most people, in the absence of a different idea, will open themselves up and pour themselves out onto the page. This unstructured, open-ended, non-directed flow of thoughts and feelings (sometimes called free writing, or flow writing, or stream of consciousness writing) uncannily parallels the process of catastrophic grief, which is in itself oceanic, endless and formless. What helps? Writing techniques that imbed structure, boundaries and form.

I've always been an advocate for choices and options in the journal. But my work with traumatic stress and catastrophic grief convinced me that for people who are in deep emotional pain, having choices is essential for feelings of mastery, comfort and manageability.

Here, then, is a cornucopia of 12 ideas and suggestions for writing your way through grief. Most of these can be accomplished in 15 minutes or less, which is helpful for two main reasons. First, when grief is new, feelings are so close to the surface and pain is so raw that short writes are less likely to pitch you into overwhelm. Second, our culture doesn't really support us in grieving, and we are expected to return to work and resume the mantle of everyday life almost immediately after even a catastrophic loss. For many people, shorter writes are friendlier and more adaptable to daily realities.

Incidentally, shorter writes don't necessarily mean you're sacrificing outcome or results. Scientific research based on the work of James Pennebaker[8] shows that brief, intense bursts of emotional release writing — only 15 minutes a day, for only four consecutive days — is correlated with increased immune system functioning that can last for several weeks. Since grief often compromises the immune system and leaves you more vulnerable to colds, flu and infection, these writes can help your physical as well as your emotional health.

1. **First things first: There aren't any rules.** Journal writing isn't like flossing; you don't have to do it every day. And it isn't school: You don't have to spell the words right, or punctuate them, or worry about grammar. Give yourself permission to write whatever comes. You're not being judged or graded by anyone else, so please don't judge or grade yourself.

2. **Choose a journal that fits your lifestyle** and feels comfy and nurturing. Some people treasure lovely blank bound books. Others favor spiral notebooks that can be chucked into a backpack. If you think at your keyboard, keep your journal on computer. There is excellent journal software available; I like LifeJournal, available at major bookstores, or on the internet (www.lifejournal.com). Or write your journal via e-mail to a support group or mailing list of chosen friends and family.

3. **Time can feel like an enemy** when you're adjusting to a loss, so it's comforting and reassuring to document your movement

---

[8] *Writing to Heal,* James W. Pennebaker, Ph.D., Oakland, CA: New Harbinger Publications, 2004.

through it. You can do this by numbering the pages of your journal and only writing on one side of the page. Or try writing in a one-year diary with pre-printed pages.

4. **Get in the habit of writing three words** that describe your feelings at the beginning and end of every journal entry. This helps you track your feelings over time and gives you an opportunity to notice that emotions shift with time and process.

5. **Set the timer and write fast and furious** for a predetermined number of minutes — 5, 10, 15 (more, if you have time, energy and desire). When the timer buzzes, close your book or file and move on. Come back as often as you wish.

6. **Because it is common for memory to be affected with acute grief,** make to-do lists, and keep them right in your journal or day planner.

7. **Make other lists, as well.** Lists are great for organizing and categorizing, and their structure is comforting when things feel like they are spinning out of control. Write lists of your emotions, memories, plans, ideas, fantasies and more.

8. **Before you go to bed,** choose something you'd like to experience the following day — a feeling of hope or pleasure; an item crossed off a to-do list; an experience such as a productive meeting or a gym workout. Write this "Choice du Jour" in your journal. As you go to sleep, reflect on your choice. How would you recognize success? What can you do to arrange your day to increase the likelihood that your choice will manifest? At night, write for five minutes reflecting on outcomes.

9. **When you are aching with longing for your loved one,** write "Captured Moments" —brief vignettes written quickly, like impressionistic sketches, of instants of time. Make them intense with vivid descriptions. Reach for sensory details — the sight, smell, touch, taste, feel of things. Include the emotional senses, too, finding precise words for feelings. A collection of Captured Moments becomes like a written photo album, preserving precious memories for all time.

10. **AlphaPoems are an easy and structured way** to get started with poetic expression. Write the alphabet, or the letters of any word or phrase, vertically down the side of your page. Then write a poem in which each successive line begins with the next letter on the page. (It's perfectly xceptable to make xceptions for xtra hard letters.) Try this even if you think you're not a poet, or that the process sounds silly. You'll likely be amazed at how easily the poem comes, and how much like a poem it actually sounds. Here's an AlphaPoem called "Grief," from Taylor's journal:

> *A crushing*
> *bellow*
> *calls from deep inside*
> *driving to be heard*
> *ever so*
> *frightening, ever so demanding,*
> *grief*
> *hits with a tornado's force,*
> *igniting the fire,*
> *jarring the senses,*
> *kicking the safety and comfort away.*
> *Lamenting the loss, the pain*
> *mere words cannot begin to describe.*

No, words cannot do justice to the
once-held, once-loved, always-remembered
passion. 'Tis
queer this experience
required in life.
Solace can be found
tonight, tomorrow—
until once again the
vine of death crawls in my
window, playing the
xylophone of harmony lost.
Yes, I will go on. You will never be
zero.

11. **Unsent Letters are an excellent way** to maintain a sense of communication with your loved one and can offer deep opportunities for soothing and comfort.

12. **Sometimes the only way** to get through devastation is to imagine a time when it might not hurt so much. Write a "One Year from Today" entry in which you fast-forward yourself to the healing side of the grief. Allow yourself a glimpse into the future. Imagine your life as if you have wheeled around through four seasons, and you are one year distant from the losses you are experiencing today

MAKING ROOM

In my mind I revisit the places you've loved,
half expecting to see you, hear your voice,
know by the tilt of your head that these
are moments you will never forget, so
I make room for them, let them fill me.

The way you waited patiently for fish,
your eyes not on the clear water of the lake,
but on the sky as it bled from crystal blue
into purple dusk, draining out between
the hills on the opposite shore, the way
you let the rest of your life fall away
in the moments before full dark.

The way your body loosened in the
presence of mountains, those spires that
marked the entrance to your cathedral,
green solitude, each breath a prayer, there
you became more you than I've ever known.

The way you laid your body at the ocean's
edge, a supplicant at the altar, the ritual
baptism by sun, salt, water, a lump of sand
rubbed into skin small penance for the
sorrow you surrendered to the dailyness of tides.

The way you dared to leave a part of yourself
in each of the places you loved, as if you knew
you'd be back to claim them, as if you were

leaving them for me, lessons in surprise and delight.
I take from these places all of the things you didn't
know how to give me, all of the things I didn't know
how to ask for, and I will pass them to my daughters,
and I will stand still and let them move me.

Amy Christman

Poetry Prompt

The poet Lisel Mueller speaks of placing her grief
"in the mouth of language." Write a poem in the
second person (the "you" voice) to someone you have
lost. List the specifics of memory and mourning.
It may help to start your stanzas "The way you...."

CHAPTER 14

Coping Strategies for Catastrophic Trauma

I read the news today, o boy.....
—John Lennon

On September 11, 2001, we were plunged into a crisis that no one could fully comprehend. Our paradigms shifted, boundaries vanished, and we were not prepared. In the words of the poet Adrienne Rich, "the maps they gave us/ were out of date by years." There were no "right" answers, no magic potions, no formulas or recipes. September 11 gave nearly everyone in America (and around the world) a consensual context for shock, horror and devastation — the same feelings that many people experience in their personal lives following private catastrophes or community traumas. Here are some common-sense suggestions for managing difficult times, written in the aftermath of September 11 and updated to reflect individually experienced trauma as well as collective disasters.

1. **Accept your emotions.** Whatever you are feeling, it is a normal and natural response. There are four basic feeling groups: Mad, sad, glad and scared. These basic groups provide the ingredients for many dozens of feelings. You might experience any number of different, and possibly conflicting, emotions, which may shift quickly and without warning. All of this, unfortunately, is to be expected and may continue for many weeks or months. It is crucially important to be able to tell the difference between feeling an emotion such as profound depression or white-hot rage and acting on an emotion, such as harming yourself or someone/something else.

2. **Tell your story.** We need to talk about catastrophe, to discharge the tension, to move it out of our bodies, to witness and be witnessed. Allow yourself to express as much as you need to, keeping in mind the need to pace yourself.

3. **Pace yourself.** Whether it is a world disaster such as September 11, a private catastrophe such as rape or auto accident, or a community trauma such as hurricane, plane crash or wildfire, be careful to pace yourself when it comes to media coverage and ruminative storytelling. Repetitive images and continual verbal analysis and speculation imbed themselves into our psyches, overstimulate our adrenal glands, and overload our mental and psychological capacities to process. Give yourself a break from endless-loop coverage, whether it be on CNN or in continued and ongoing reliving of the trauma through repeated telling to curious, concerned friends and family.

4. **Find your tribe.** Community is vitally important in times of crisis. Humans are tribal people. Find your tribe, whether that is family, friends, church, school or classes, workplace, support

group, volunteer activities, e-mail listservs, neighborhood, one good friend. Have at least one source of support that reliably gives you contact with caring, accepting human beings.

5. **Relentless self-care is mandatory.** Even in the midst of excruciating trauma, it is not always possible to take time out from our own individual lives. We must continue going to school, going to work, feeding our children, driving carpool, and living our lives against a ghastly backdrop of grief, fear and uncertainty. It is essential that we practice relentless self-care. Get enough sleep; if you can't sleep, at least try to rest peacefully. Eat in a way that feeds and fuels your body. Get some exercise. Do whatever comforts and sustains you: Hot baths, hikes, time with friends, time alone, hobbies, movies, weekends away. Some people (extraverts) get their batteries recharged by being with other people. Others (introverts) recharge their batteries by being alone. Know what fuels you, and do that relentlessly.

6. **Take care of your body.** Move tension and accumulated feelings and toxins out of your body. Sweating, elimination and bodywork are three good ways. Exercise, saunas or steam rooms, massage, yoga, eating simple foods simply prepared, drinking lots of water, and breathing will help.

7. **Beauty heals.** "Let the beauty that you love be what you do," says the 14th century mystic poet Rumi. If you love the outdoors, be in nature. If you love art, go to the art museum or get out your paints. If you love music, surround yourself with the most beautiful music you can find. If you love flowers, buy or plant them for yourself. Surround yourself with beauty.

8. **Eat a poem.** Former US Poet Laureate Billy Collins said, in the aftermath of September 11, "Comfort can be found in just about any poem. I'm going to go read the Psalms." Find a poem that speaks to you of hope or grief or courage, and chew it up. Read it over and over. Let certain lines digest in you until you find yourself thinking of them in odd times throughout your day. Let this poem live inside you and guide you to your own True North.

9. **Pray.** Whatever your religious or spiritual persuasion (including not being sure if you have one), examine whether you essentially believe in a benevolent power that is beyond your personal self. It matters less what you call it (God, Goddess, Spirit, Nature, Jesus, Buddha, Allah, the Source, Infinity, Life Energy, the Divine) than that you feel it as a positive presence for good. Prayer, like so much else, is a highly individualized expression that may or may not involve the formal rituals of bowed head, silence, closed eyes, composed speech. For many people, turning to prayer is one antidote to feeling helpless. If you already have a spiritual practice, now is the time to deepen and extend it.

10. **Be kind.** Go out of your way to extend kindness in small, everyday ways. Make space for the car in front of you to change lanes. Smile at the grocery store clerk. Thank a fireman or policeman for the work they do. Extend friendship and support to a stranger. In the aftermath of 9/11, the brilliant poet Maya Angelou said of the many deaths, "We must not see this as 3,000 lives lost. We must see this as one precious life lost, and we must see that 3,000 times." Some people committed to witness each individual death by performing 3,000 acts of

intentional kindness, or performing 3,000 hours of volunteer service. Love is the one sure antidote to hatred.

11. **Write a journal.** It is well documented that writing your thoughts and feelings during times of trauma and distress is a healing, nurturing, effective means of release. Be sure to date your entries, and stop if you begin to feel overwhelmed. There are no rules; you don't need to write a certain number of pages, or for a certain length of time. Even five or ten minutes every now and then is helpful. If you don't know where to start, begin with the story you are living in that moment. "Right now I feel…." or "Today I am…" will get you going. Then just tell yourself a story.

12. **Ask for help.** If you cannot bear the trauma alone, and particularly if you struggled with depression or anxiety before the crisis, ask for professional help when you need it. Psychotherapists, social workers, counselors, employee assistance programs, psychologists, psychiatrists, clergy, lay ministers, expressive arts therapists and many other mental health professionals are trained and ready to companion you through these hard times. There is compassionate help available. Don't hesitate to ask for it.

MIRACLES YOU MIGHT MISS

Praise the mutilated world
and the gray feather a thrush lost,
and the gentle light that strays and vanishes
and returns.
> — *Adam Zagajewski*
> *"Try to Praise the Mutilated World"*

Try to praise the mutilated world,
there are miracles you might miss otherwise.

Each night, the tiny death of sleep
we cannot live without, each day
the way people push up against
each other's edges, the quick heat
of anger, both just and unjust,
the sour aftertaste of regret, and
the giddy surprise of a hand extended
in apology, in gratitude, in supplication.

The prickly smell of rotting garbage,
the discarded and unwanted that strengthens
the soil when turned over as compost.

The way deep furrows fill slowly with water,
lakes born from jagged cuts in the earth's
soft face, teeming later with life.

The way moss pulls itself over a fallen
tree like a bright blanket, the image of

comfort and warmth, when underneath
is a riot of decay and decomposition,
the fallen returning to where they began,
making room for something else to begin.

The way a wound oozes pus in order
to cleanse itself, and the scabbing over,
the itchy healing and joining of tissues,
the way the body wages fierce and silent
war with itself, and you, always the winner.

Amy Christman

Poetry Prompt

Write a praise poem of your gratitudes.

INTUITION AND SPIRITUALITY

CHAPTER 15

Journal of a Synchronicity

June 5, 2001

Today as I was rooting around in the uppermost closet shelves, the "Time 2 Move" sweatshirt fell on my head. It always gives me pause when it surfaces; since 1989 it has been the harbinger of change. It disappears for years at a time and then shows up when I'm ready for a major life event. I put it on and sat on the edge of the bed, musing about the changes it has foreshadowed.

I have wondered for a while if it is "time 2 move" from this apartment where I've lived happily and contentedly for a dozen years. Maybe I'm finally ready to be a homeowner again.

June 10

Had brunch with Marta and Leigh today. I mentioned my restlessness and desire to buy a place. Hearing myself say it out loud made it more tangible and real. They were enthusiastic and supportive.

June 11

As I was sorting through my mail I noticed a real estate ad with a townhouse listed by Lois, who I saw at the high school reunion last summer. It reminded me that I had spoken with her briefly a year ago about the possibility of buying something. At the time it seemed too overwhelming — prices just seemed out of reach. Now, of course, they're even higher. Argh.

June 12

I drove by the townhouse and it's in a great location. Looks very much like the last place I owned, which I loved. Called Lois to ask for a showing. It's under contract. She told me to get prequalified for a loan. I discovered realtor.com, which lets me do my own market research and gives addresses I can drive by. I also filled out a loan application on line. The fact that I'm self-employed apparently could make it more complicated.

June 15

Have been consumed with looking at the outsides of places and am rapidly educating myself on what is and is not acceptable. There is some unbelievable crap selling for ridiculous prices. One townhouse has a master bedroom balcony that overlooks railroad tracks no more than 20 feet away. I know these tracks; six or eight freight trains a day go through. Charming. Many townhouse complexes are built around acres of asphalt parking lots. I looked at a place that had beautiful grounds and a "detached" garage — extremely detached, about 100 yards down a significant hill. I can just imagine how much fun that would be in the winter! Anything I buy would have to have covered parking and trees. I can't bear the thought of living in the midst of an asphalt and concrete jungle.

June 18

Leave for the women's retreat tomorrow. Today in writing group, Joy closed with an ee cummings poem which she recited from memory, the one about the leaping greenly spirits of trees and a blue true dream of sky. I love the way she recites, so compelling and dramatic. It makes me want to drop everything and memorize poems.

June 22

Day of Silence at women's retreat. I am so in love with the trees here at Benet Pines. The weather has been exquisite, a blue true dream of sky. Found the ee cummings poem on the internet and broke silence this evening by reading it into the circle. It starts out:

> *i thank You God for most this amazing*
> *day: for the leaping greenly spirits of trees*
> *and a blue true dream of sky; and for everything*
> *which is natural which is infinite which is yes*
>
> *i who have died am alive again today.....*

July 19

I find myself saying the cummings poem over and over in my head. I wake up every morning and my first conscious thought is *i who have died am alive again today.* This poem is living in my body. I am eating it. I know this process. Like the "Time 2 Move" sweatshirt, this is a harbinger of change. Poetic magic is afoot.

July 25

Looked at a darling townhouse in perfect condition, but claustrophobically small and woefully expensive. First time I've actually connected with a realtor through this process. I'm the first one to see this place. She assured me it will not be on the market more than a week and encouraged me to act swiftly if I want it. I told her I'm leaving town tomorrow and am probably not a candidate. I'm prequalified for a loan that size, but the mortgage payment would be quite a bit higher than I'm comfortable with.

July 31
Back from teaching at the poetry therapy intensive. I can't shake the cummings poem. I'm making it August's Poem of the Month at journaltherapy.com.

August 5
Woke up this morning with the cummings poem in my head and the brilliant awareness that maybe I'm looking in the wrong zip codes. Checked out the neighborhoods a bit south, between where I am now and the office, and sure enough, it looks like there's a significant difference in asking price.

August 6
Today I connected with a lawyer who is selling his condo himself, and it is affordable, and it has all the things I absolutely positively can't live without — especially trees! Mature trees, gorgeous trees, leaping greenly spirits of trees, old-growth trees, beautiful grounds, a front porch, my own garden area, covered parking, good location halfway between my family and my office, possibility for community with neighbors, quiet neighborhood, a good gym nearby, across the street from Crown Hill Lake and the wetlands preserve, a neighborhood grocer on the corner. And the leaping greenly spirits of trees! Oh those trees …. they call to me.

Walking through the breezeway into the interior of the complex is like being transported to Oz. It goes from a pleasant but utterly nondescript exterior to a magical fairyland of forest-in-the-city. Flowers, shrubs, trees, trees, trees.

August 7

Well, I have spent practically the entire day bonding with my new condo, checking out the leaping greenly spirits of trees and especially sneaking peeks at the individual gardens. There are some ferocious gardeners there — the whole place has this rampant, overgrown, fertile, fecund, wildly creative feeling to it. There are hardwood trees mixed in with the pines and aspen, so fall should be glorious. I who have died am alive again today!

August 9

I bought it. Earnest money, contract, loan approval, whole enchilada.

August 31

The closing is at noon today. I am a homeowner! Thank you ee cummings for reaching out across time and space to land in me a poem that guided me to my own true home. It is Time 2 Move!

I WAKE WITHOUT RISING

I am waiting for the day to shake me
gasping, to fling me on the shore
of possibility, a slick fish arching
with purpose against the plane of sky,
gills beating a staccato rhythm, poised
to dive and surface, and dive again into the
everyday necessity of doing. I am waiting
for the tide of too little sleep to creep away
from the shore of my laziness, the bared sand
imprinted with the litany of chores that call
with the sharp insistence of gulls: fold the
laundry; empty the dishwasher; weed the
garden; thaw, season and roast the chicken;
sweep and dust, straighten and put away.
Work, now, becomes the alarm, the shrill
voice calling, against which I measure the
comfort of these down pillows, these body-warm
sheets, the presence of your breathing. I wake
without rising, drifting in the slow current of imagining
a day I can fill with pleasures of my own choosing.

Amy Christman

Poetry Prompt

Synchronicity often involves patient awareness,
a watchful waiting, noticing the mundane details
of daily life while staying open to possibilities.
Write a poem that starts out, "I am waiting for...."

CHAPTER 16

Five Ways to Scribe Your Intuition

After nearly 20 years as a journal therapist, I know there are dozens of good reasons to write things down. But none intrigues, delights or satisfies me more consistently than giving written form to the still, small voice inside — the voice of intuition.

So grab your notebook, blank book, clean computer screen, legal pad, or whatever you write on (remember, it doesn't matter what it is, as long as it feels comfy) and let's explore five ways to scribe your intuition. Don't worry about "rules" like spelling, grammar, or if you're doing it "right." In my journal universe, the only "rule" is allegiance to your own soul and spirit.

1. **Keep an intuition log.** New to the intuition game? Not even sure how to recognize that still, small voice? Start by noticing. Be an intuition detective, gathering clues to what might be intuitive flashes or hits. Just as you might write down five gratitudes at the end of each day, try writing five experiences,

thoughts or "random" events that might have been intuition. Be sure to note your body's response. Did you experience a "pop" or "aha" of recognition, like a lightbulb over your head? Was it a stirring in your tummy? Was it an opening and softening of your heart? Did you get goose bumps? You'll quickly learn to recognize your own "felt-sense" of intuition.

2. **Get curious about patterns.** Angeles Arrien says, "If something knocks on your door three times, answer the door." A client of mine — let's call him Jeff — described to me a sensation in his body, near his gut, "that feels like a hole but is not a wound." Based on the conversation we were having, I said, "Sounds like it might be a yearning." A strange look came over Jeff's face. He said, "That's funny. All week I've had the chorus of an old Supremes song running through my head — 'I've got that yearning, burning feeling inside me' — and just yesterday, somebody told me I reminded him of someone who was yearning for redemption."

    "Get to a clean page in your notebook," I said. "Give me five minutes on yearning. Write everything you know. Ready, set, go." As Jeff discovered in the write, his intuition was guiding him back to an earlier life experience that wanted to be embraced, explored and expanded.

3. **Pay attention to the perfection of "mistakes."** Eleanor was feeling mad at herself when she arrived at Monday afternoon writing group. She had just come from a bon voyage party for a friend who was moving away. Eleanor's assignment for the celebration had been to bring helium balloons. Because she couldn't see out her rear-view mirror with the balloons bouncing around in her back seat, she pulled over en route and put them in the trunk.

She arrived at the park where the party was being held, scooping up purse and packages as she exited the car. But when she opened the trunk, juggling her armload of stuff, the balloons escaped and floated away. She watched, helpless, as her beautiful bouquet of well-wishes wafted heavenward.

Of course in the end it didn't matter a whit, and the party was just as lovely with the thought of balloons as with the balloons themselves. But Eleanor still felt abashed.

"What if there's a bigger story here?" I asked her. "What's your Higher Self trying to tell you?" And she wrote:

I wanted the balloons to make people smile, and I realize that my story caused lots of smiles…. I'm sure there is also a message for me to stop berating myself and telling myself "how stupid I can be" …. Releasing the balloons that said "Best wishes" and "Good luck" seems now to be like a prayer that I have held in my heart for the world. I have had this wish and said this prayer to myself so many times as I hear of the sadness and tragedy in the world…. Perhaps this is God's way of telling me that my thoughts and prayers released with a loving intent is all that the Divine Power needs to make this world a better place. And my intuition tells me that I must not berate myself with the idea that what I do is so little compared to what needs to be done. It says that once I release the loving thoughts, they can spread far and wide, ending up somewhere I can't even imagine, just like the balloons.

4. **Be a scribe for the still, small voice inside.** Recently I was frustrated to bits with a business project that just wasn't flowing. No matter how much I tried to stay fluid and open to guidance, I found myself stopped at every turn. Each time I hit the wall, I did an intuition check — asking inside if this project was the right thing to be doing, and if this was the right time to

be doing it. I consistently got "green light" answers, which made the discontinuity with my experience even more baffling.

Finally, in utter exasperation, I sat down with my journal. "What is it that I'm not seeing here?" I asked myself, and then I got quiet and sat in silence. Although I had written about this situation many times, I knew there had to be something deeper that I was missing. Slowly, words began to form in my mind. I wrote them down, at first haltingly, then more quickly. Within ten minutes, I knew what had been eluding me. The project was in fact right, and the timing was also right. But there was one element of the project that needed a subtle shift. Once my intuition pointed it out to me, I instantly saw the enormity of the positive difference that subtle shift would make. So I committed to it, revisioned the project accordingly, and immediately found myself back in flow.

5. **If words won't come, try drawing or collage.** Sometimes intuition would rather speak in symbols than in English. Jane, an artist who is struggling to liberate herself from a marriage that feels like a slow death, writes:

    Last night, late, after working really hard on something, I was about to fall into bed and decided instead that I felt too separated from my art. I thought I would take just a few minutes and make something, to reconnect. At first I just smudged colors and made a background. At that point I was going to put it away and save it for another project, but I decided instead to draw abstract lines. I drew a few and felt awkward about it. Thought, well, the paper's ruined now anyway, I might as well keep going. I drew a shape I thought looked really dumb. Kept going anyway. When I had just about filled up the whole thing I put down the pastels and thought, now WHAT am I going to do with this. Can I somehow salvage that pretty background? Erase the lines? Cut it up for collage?

I stepped back about three paces and looked at it again, and had the wind knocked out of me. It was a bird, as clear as can be. Not a literally interpreted bird, but a sort of primitive interpretation of a bird. I had drawn a top knot on its head, even, and not realized it was a bird. I have to tell you it gave me the chills. So then I sat right down and wrote to my most ardently skeptical artist friend about it, ...and uploaded a scan to her. Finally went to bed, wondering if I had been touched by something or other, or if I was imagining things. This morning I got up to find a post from above-noted skeptical friend. Here's what she said. "Jane. It's the phoenix."

Now THAT gave me chills. I went to read the myth of the phoenix, and how only one ever lives and when it senses its oncoming death it goes to its nest, sets itself aflame, sings as it burns, and a new phoenix arises from the ashes. Yikes. It's hard to think I was not touched by something.

It certainly does seem as if Jane were touched by something — something that is reaching out to touch each one of us. Every day our souls reach out and speak to us from ancient mythic realms, assuring us that we are profoundly loved, that we are astonishingly wise, and that communication with our own deepest knowing is as close as the next clean page or clean screen of our journals.

SOMETHING LIKE LIGHT STANDS UP*

* from the poem "Poem White Page White Page Poem"
by Muriel Rukeyser

Something stands up in me and is alive,
something like the shouting of crows,
raucous and rollicking, urgency in slick
light dancing off bright feathers.
Something like the bold rise of dark
trees, hot secrets cloaked in rough skin,
shadow selves spread like soft webs at my feet.
Something stands up like the luminous curl
of wave on its way to loud rejoicing,
incandescence spread on the rough edge
of sand, the taking in and giving back.
Something is moving in me, is dancing
like wind in the dry tops of marsh grasses,
this arid whisper that sounds something
like truth, stands up in me, and is alive.

Amy Christman

Poetry Prompt

Intuition is often described as a light bulb going off,
a "pop" or "flash" or felt-sense that stands up and
demands attention. Think about a time when you had a
clear sense of intuition. Write a poem in which you
describe the visceral, physical experience of intuition
as the "something" that stands up in you.

CHAPTER 17

Riding the Inky Wave

There is a story from Jewish mysticism that my friend and poetry therapy colleague Sister Arleen Hynes tells[9] about a man who received a message in a dream that a great treasure awaited him. He was to journey at once to a village many days' travel away, where a sentry would tell him where to find his treasure.

The man set out immediately, and after long days and nights of perilous travel he indeed reached the village. Just as the dream foretold, the sentry greeted him with instructions. "Return to your own village at once," the sentry said, "and when you get there, dig under your hearth."

This was the treasure he had traveled so far to claim? Disillusioned and embittered, and without resources for even one night's lodging, the man began the treacherous journey home. He finally reached

---

9 *Biblio/Poetry Therapy: The Interactive Handbook,* Arleen Hynes & Mary Hynes-Berry, St. Paul: North Star Press, 1994.

his village, bone tired and despairing. He entered his stone-cold hut. Left only with the shards of his broken dreams, the man wanted nothing more than to build a fire and warm himself. Yet against all hope he used the last of his strength to brush the ashes from the hearth and dig beneath it. And there he found his treasure.

The story is timeless and universal. Throughout the eons man sets off on quests to find the elusive treasure that will make him whole and complete. Along the way there are dragons to slay, battles to fight, perils to survive, noble deeds to do. The quest always ends the same way: The answer, the treasure, has been his all along.

For many, the most transformative moment in personal journal keeping is the awareness that spirituality is available right now, and it can be acknowledged, recognized, created, explored and experienced in the pages of a notebook.

If you have yearned for deeper meaning and purpose to your life, consider the possibility that a private relationship with your own spirituality could be the treasure buried under your own hearth. And your journal is an excellent place to dig.

Entering the Silence

Spiritual connection in your journal begins with silence. Find a place where you can filter out distractions. When I was small, I took literally the directive from Jesus to "go into the closet and pray." Now I just unplug the phone.

It's nice to clear your space of clutter, but don't wait to try these ideas until you've cleaned your desk. Power objects such as stones, shells, crystals, feathers, drums or rattles can help you attain a meditative state, especially if there's a story behind how you found or received them.

If you practice yoga, tai chi, qi gong or another movement meditation, do this before writing. If you don't, start with slow and gentle stretching. This releases tension and grounds you in your body.

Breathe deeply into your abdomen — your center — in full, rhythmic cycles. Not only does this oxygenate your cells, but breathwork is a necessity for depth of spiritual awareness.

Mantra/Crystals

Ira Progoff's work with written process meditation suggests seven-syllable "mantra/crystals" drawn from the context of the individual's life history.

> *In making the mantra/crystal, we are seeking merely to put a small, representative piece [of the experience] into words in a way that will recall us to the atmosphere of the original experience…. There is apparently a factor of inner wisdom that expresses itself at the depth of human beings whenever the circumstances are right for it, and this factor seems to have a direct affinity for the seven-syllable mantra/crystals. I infer that the seven-syllable form and rhythm reflects an inherent cycle in the natural world, and therefore it easily comes into harmony with the principle of inner wisdom that is present at the depth levels of the human psyche.[10]*

---

10 *The Practice of Process Meditation*, Ira Progoff, New York: Dialogue House, 1981. This book is out of print; used and collectible copies are available at amazon.com and half.com. Much of the original text has been assimilated into the new edition of Progoff's *At a Journal Workshop* published by J.P. Tarcher.

In addition to the prescribed length, Progoff suggests that the chosen phrase be smooth and rhythmic "so that we can easily speak and repeat them under our breath…. without conscious effort or thought." The mantra/crystal should correspond to your individual breath pattern so that you can fit the entire phrase into one cycle of breathing in and breathing out. Progoff emphasizes the benefit of gerunds (verbs ending in -*ing*) because of their inherent movement and flow.

The construction of mantra/crystals from your own life experience is both complex and subtle, and I refer you to *The Practice of Process Meditation* for the full treatment. The essential question to ask is, *Where does it place me in my inner space?* If your mantra/crystal reflects a statement, idea, conscious belief or doctrine, it will draw you into the mental realm, Progoff cautions. "Choose an image, therefore, a symbol, a metaphor, since these can move about naturally in the twilight range like fish in the oceanic waters." Some examples of seven-syllable mantra/crystals from Progoff's work follow.

> *Letting the Self become still*
> *Holding the stillness within*
> *Feeling the movement of life*
> *The river flows to the sea*
> *Knowing the goodness of God*
> *Feeling the love of the Lord*
> *Feeling the pain of my life*
> *The morning song of the birds*
> *I and my Father are one*

Keep your journal before you as you silently speak your mantra/crystal to the rhythm of your breath. Notice any images, symbols, feelings, colors or awarenesses. Write them down in simple words or phrases: "Flash of orange/gold in dark tunnel." "Peace, calm, tears." "Ocean wave." You can open your eyes just slightly enough to see, or you can try holding your left index finger (reverse if you are left-handed) lightly above the tip of your pen and writing with your eyes closed.

Writing as Meditation

Writing becomes a meditation when you bring your total awareness and gratitude to the act. When you have fully entered the silence, bring your attention to your journal. Become aware that Spirit moving through you is actively creating something that is unique in all the world and that did not exist even a moment ago. Michael speaks to this phenomenon:

> When I write in my journal, I affix ink onto paper, resulting in a visual display which can be returned to over and over again. I have begun to ask myself the questions: What do I want to make now? What might I want to see/read in the future? Is what I am creating now in the service of my wants? And so I have been attending to not only content, but also form, and sprinkling my pages with symbols which remind me of the sacredness of my practice: hearts, simple mandalas, the star of David, exclamation points, question marks and spirals. I've become freer with paper, too, double-spacing for visual effect and occasionally just leaving a page with a word or two on it — a statement of simplicity and significance.

When you feel ready, take a deep breath and begin a written meditation. It doesn't matter where you start. Begin with an awareness that came to you in the silence. Or imagine yourself in your special place in nature. Or remember a time when you experienced a moment of grace or bliss.

Allow yourself to simply write. Suspend judgment about whether you're doing it right. If you come to a natural pause in your writing, go back and reread what you've already written. Your writing will often spontaneously continue.

When you are writing from your spiritual center, it feels effortless. Words flow freely. Storytelling becomes natural and fluid. You may feel as if you are in an altered state of consciousness, where time is elastic and acuity is sharpened. You may feel expansive and connected to the unity of all things. There is often a sense of gratitude, peace of mind and clarity. You are riding the inky wave.

I Cast a Wide Net

I cast a wide net into these deep waters.
Standing on the shore, thick and solid
as a curve of thigh, I raise my arms in
slick surrender, release that dark
circle, its necklace of weights
bright sparks as it rises, spinning.
The cobalt sky is divided,
multiplied into knotted segments.
I am stunned into stillness, giddy with the
turning, the graceful descent, the settling
onto the rippled surface of the bay,
the sinking. There is a rhythm
to this searching, toss, spin, drop,
drag, my hand, my arms, the net
come up empty again and again.
Neon fishes skim the sandy bottom,
sense the drift of net before they see it,
dart into the shadows beyond its soft grip.
The empty net is heavy going home,
the weight of water and chances missed,
but there are bright scales on the rough hemp
that sing loudly of presence and hope.
I long to tuck one under my tongue,
learn to feed in half-darkness,
sleep with my eyes open,
to see what it is I am missing.

Amy Christman

Poetry Prompt

Dive deep beneath the inky wave. Gather images,
thoughts, awarenesses, insights, intuitions that come to
you in meditation and write them in poetic language.

CHAPTER 18

Unseen Companions

One December, in the midst of the darkest nights of the year, I experienced a dark night of the soul. My faith was seriously tested. I struggled with a profound sense of separation from God. Like the psalmist David, "I cry by day, but thou dost not answer; and by night, but find no rest." (Psalms 22:2)

Dark night or no, life goes on. One day I stopped by the neighborhood bookstore to pick up a few Christmas gifts. Twenty minutes later, loaded chest-high with books, I headed to the sales counter. The aisles were narrow, the crowds jostled, and suddenly a book came sailing through the air and landed face-up in my arms.

"I'm terribly sorry!" cried the woman with whom I'd collided. "Let me put that away!" As she reached for the book, I glanced down. On the cover was Abbott Handerson Thayer's painting *Angel*, which I remembered from my college humanities class. The book was called *Ask Your Angels*. I laughed out loud. "That's okay," I told the apologetic "angel" who caused the book to fly into my waiting heart. "I'll just get it."

That serendipitous event began a magical, mystical journey through my dark night of the soul. I began "asking my angels" in journal dialogue, Unsent Letters and written meditation and prayer. And, no surprise, I immediately began hearing answers.

Angels, guides, muses, the spirits of beloved ones who have passed on, the Holy Ghost, patron saints, Christ Consciousness, nature, devas, the Soul, the Wise Ones, intuition, Higher Self ... all of these are unseen companions whose support and guidance are available for the asking. The journal is a wonderfully eclectic melting pot for unseen companions. It doesn't matter what you call them, or if you call them anything at all. Just ask for their guidance. Then wait for the answer. Write whatever comes.

It may seem odd, foreign, or unsettling to communicate with unseen companions, but Alma Daniel and her coauthors of *Ask Your Angels*[11] assure us it's perfectly natural:

> Contact and conversation with your angel is filled with all the tenderness, love and wonderment of discovering a best friend. Talking with angels is an entirely natural relationship, although over the centuries it's become obscured by the belief that if you can't see something or touch it — it isn't real.

The Inner Wisdom dialogue is the communication technique of choice for most experienced spiritual journalkeepers. Begin with an opening ritual in which you create sacred space. This can be as simple as clearing your desk or table and lighting a candle. Add any

---

[11] *Ask Your Angels*, Alma Daniel, Timothy Wyllie, Andrew Ramer, New York: Wellspring/Ballantine, 1992.

other elements of your personal spiritual practice, such as prayer, chanting, symbol systems such as runes or tarot cards, hymns or sacred music, altars, or any other deepening devices.

Then enter a meditative state in which you consciously call in your unseen companions. It may be helpful to visualize yourself in a beautiful place in nature, or another realm where you can open yourself to connection. Ask sincerely and openly for the wisdom and grace of your unseen companion to enter you and speak to you.

When you are ready, formulate a question that your heart wants to know. Wait in patient silence for guidance and inspiration. It may be helpful to formulate a list of questions before you enter the meditation.

Allow plenty of time. The Inner Wisdom dialogue often unfolds in waves or layers interspersed with periods of silence. Usually after a few exchanges, the dialogue will find its own direction.

The Inner Wisdom dialogue technique comes directly out of the teachings of the late Dr. Ira Progoff. It remains one of the most enduring and beautiful legacies of this brilliant man. As you communicate with your unseen companions, offer a message of gratitude to Dr. Progoff, and ask your angel to pass it along to his soul.

THIS WAY

The sleepy hush of early woods,
breathing, shadows like aged lace,
the trickle and drip of leftover rain
like a voice close to the ear telling you,
this is the way, this fallen maple slick
with moss, this gloss of amber puddle,
this perfect circle of powdery morels,
this is the way to approach your life.
Infuse it with quiet beauty, search beneath
all the stones, guide your happiness by
stars and the way the wind bends
the wild tops of pines. This
is the way, this race that slows
to the soft press of pond against
the low shoulder of muddy shore,
this trip into leaf green light.

Amy Christman

Poetry Prompt

The voice of Spirit is often heard in the natural world.
Write a poem about a place in nature — an actual place
you go, a place you have been, or a place that exists
when you close your eyes and conjure up a beautiful
place — where you can be still and hear the voices
of angels or other unseen companions.

Saying Goodbye, Saying Hello

CHAPTER 19

Saying Goodbye, Saying Hello

One of my favorite annual rituals takes place over the last few days of December. I surround myself with my journal volumes for the year and read them through. Then I write a summary of the year, noting the highlights and low points, the realized visions and the places of disappointment, challenge or heartache. I linger over moments I want to savor and reflect on lessons learned. When I have steeped myself in the immediate past, I look ahead to the blank pages of the new year. I set down my visions and dreams, my goals and intentions, with as much specificity as possible, making sure to ground my visions in "current reality" — the place from which I embark.

I perform this annual ritual when the calendar changes, in the shortest days of the year. Others prefer to do annual review around their birthdays, or at the summer solstice. Here is a model you might find useful. It is not necessary to do all of the steps in the reviewing section, although the visioning section works best when all steps are

undertaken, in order. Allow plenty of time for this. I usually set aside
two or three hours a day for several consecutive days.

The Year in Review

Highlights & Challenges
Divide a page into two columns. On the left, head the column
"Highlights." On the right, "Challenges." Make a list of the "best of"
and "worst of" the year just past — the highlights and challenges, the
good news and bad news. Write quickly. Don't censor or edit. Get
creative — include individual moments as well as larger themes.

Highlights
Review your "Highlights" column. What have been some of the
stand-out gifts and highlights of the closing year? How have you
received and responded to these gifts? Which have you welcomed
and accepted? Which have you had difficulty receiving? Which were
planned, and which were unplanned?

Challenges
Review your "Challenges" column. What have been some of the
most difficult challenges of the closing year? How have you met
these challenges? Which ways of meeting them have been effective?
Which have been less effective?

Gifts & Blessings
What unexpected, unimagined gifts and blessings have you received?
How has Spirit spoken to you through these gifts? In what ways
have you been a gift or blessing of Spirit to someone else?

Lessons

What have been the greatest lessons of the year just past? How responsive have you been to these lessons? What in your personal history do these lessons echo or extend?

Captured Moment

Choose any single moment from the year that moved you, and capture it in poetry or prose. It may be helpful to refer to the Highlights list, or to cluster some of the moments that stand out for you.

Goal Review

What did you set as goals, visions, intentions one year ago? Review your goals and visions. What movement have you made? How do you feel about what has or has not been accomplished?

Recap

Chronologically reconstruct the year, month by month. Use your appointment book, calendar, checkbook, etc. as reminders. Bring in news events from the outside world and other markers. Year-in-review magazine and newspaper articles are excellent sources to help you match personal experiences with national/world events.

Setting Visions for the New Year

Vision

What do you want to be, do and have in the new year? Be as specific as you can, without becoming attached to the specificity. ("I'd like to change careers" isn't very specific. "I want a new career that fulfills my creativity, serves as an inspiration to others and makes at least $60,000/year" is more specific.)

Current Reality
Taking each of your visions in turn, what is your "current reality"? Describe your present, immediate circumstances with regard to this vision. Stay objective and nonjudgmental.

Building the Bridge
What will it take to move from Current Reality to Vision? For each vision, itemize the specific actions, skills, resources it will take to actualize the vision from your current starting place.

Making the Map
Now map out by quarter and/or month the specific action steps that will help you actualize this vision. It is sometimes helpful to work backwards from the goal. Break it into manageable steps and stages, with target dates.

Accountability
Who in your life might serve as an accountability partner? This would be someone with whom you could share your vision and map, and who would be available to you to help structure your movement toward the vision.

One Year From Today
Write a journal entry dated December 31, or the eve of the annual review, in which you look back on your visions and celebrate your successful achievements. Be sure to note how you did it, the resources and support you had along the way, and how it feels to be complete.

NEW YEAR 2002

The dream changes at midnight
when I begin to peel the year
like ripe fruit, letting old
mistakes and bitter regrets fall
away in cupped segments like rough
rind. I hold tight to the intent
to master this annual birth, this
time learning to forgive the old
wounds, celebrate the common joys.
It takes a gentle hand to undo
the layers, bare the tender flesh
and never damage beyond a bruise.
There is little time for standing
still. I move into the new year
sticky and fragrant with the scent
of earth and sun and hope on my
hands, and the urge to mix tart
pulp with sweet cream, letting
the juice drip from my fingers
and chin without apology.

Amy Christman

Poetry Prompt

Write your visions for the new year in the form
of a poem. Post it on your refrigerator or
bathroom mirror and read it every day.

Journal Toolbox

AlphaPoem. A perennial favorite. Write the alphabet, A-Z or any other collection of letters) vertically down the side of a page. Then write a poem in which each successive line begins with the next letter.

Artmaking. Gives form, shape and color to personal symbolism, emotions, attitudes and thoughts. Keep simple materials, such as crayons, felt-tip markers, colored pencils, and collage supplies accessible.

Captured Moments. Vignettes capturing the sensations of particularly meaningful or emotional experiences. Written from the senses with strong descriptions. Usually one or two paragraphs.

Character Sketch. A written portrait of another person or of a part of the self.

Clustering. Also called mind-mapping or webbing. Clustering is visual free association around a central word or phrase. Lines and circles connect key thoughts and associations to the central core. A brief writing to synthesize findings may follow.

Community Journal. An ongoing communication book kept interactively with family members, caregivers or housemates.

Dialogue. An imaginary conversation written in two or more voices. On the page, it looks like a movie or play script.

Dreamwork. Writing down dreams is the first step to journal dreamwork. From there, any number of techniques can be used for self-interpretation.

Five- or Ten-Minute Writing Sprints. Timed writes designed to bring focus and intensity in short bursts.

Free Write (Stream of Consciousness). This unstructured, unboundaried, free-form narrative writing starts anywhere and goes where it pleases. Although it is the default technique for most journal writers, it is not necessarily the most effective. If you find yourself pulling away from your journal because your free writes feel disturbing or distressing, try a different technique, perhaps one with more structure — a Sprint, or a List, or a Structured Write.

Inner Wisdom/Inner Healer. A way to reliably connect with that "still, small voice" that speaks truth when we turn within.

Lists. Staccato, linear organization of thoughts, ideas, and tasks.

Lists of 100. A list on a predetermined theme or topic with 100 entries, some or many of which are likely to be repetitious.

Perspectives. An alteration in point of view that provides a different perspective on an event or a situation. For instance, you may write from a point in time in the past or the future, actually dating your page with a different month and/or year. Or you may write in the voice of someone or something else, as if he/she/it were writing in his/her/its journal about *you.*

Sentence Stems. A sentence completion process. Fill in the blank with a word or phrase. A gentle and safe way to get started writing about a difficult issue.

Springboard. A topic sentence or question written at the beginning of a journal entry to help focus and clarity the writing, usually followed by a Free Write or Writing Sprint. As a general rule, Springboards written as statements or Sentence Stems seem to stimulate thoughts and opinions, whereas Springboards written as questions tend to stimulate feelings and wonderings.

Structured Write. A series of Sentence Stems grouped and sequenced to reveal consistently deepening layers of information and awareness.

Unsent Letter. Besides Free Writing, the most common journal technique. A metaphoric communication to another that is written with the specific intention that it will not be shared with the designated audience.

For detailed information on these techniques, see <u>*Journal to the Self*</u> *and/or* <u>*The Way of the Journal,*</u> *2nd Ed.*

Acknowledgments

Heartfelt thanks to…..

My family, for endless love and support; Valerie Rickel, for inviting my columns; Amy Christman, for saying yes; Mary Caprio, for beautiful design and effortless production; Dana Reynolds, angel and muse; Linda Hendrick, for bringing elegance and artistry to business management; Joy Sawyer, wonderful teaching partner and friend; my Certified Poetry/Journal Therapist (CPT) trainees, for loving this book in manuscript form; all the Journal to the Self Certified Instructors, who extend the work to future generations; my students and clients, who tell me their stories; Collective Journey, my online writing community; my colleagues in the National Association for Poetry Therapy; Michael Geske, Gillian Wood and Robert McCarter, for true heroism; and Steve Malloy, for finding me twice.

About the Author

Kathleen (Kay) Adams LPC, RPT-MS is a psychotherapist and journal/poetry therapist in private practice. In 1985 she founded, and has continuously directed, the Center for Journal Therapy in Denver, Colorado. She offers Instructor Certification Training for the Journal to the Self workshop, as well as a two-year structured distance learning program that results in qualification for the Certified Poetry/Journal Therapist (CPT) credential. With Joy Sawyer, Kay teaches a curriculum in Writing & Healing for a Master of Arts program at the University of Denver's University College. She is Past President of the National Association for Poetry Therapy (2001-2003) and Past President of the NAPT Foundation (1997-2001). Kay is a Registered Poetry/Journal Therapist, an approved Mentor/Supervisor, and recipient of NAPT's Distinguished Service Award (1998) and Unique Award (2003). *Scribing the Soul* is her sixth book on therapeutic writing. She is working on her first novel.

About the Poet

Amy Christman, MLS, is a librarian and poet, and is currently nearing completion of her training as a Certified Poetry Therapist. She has facilitated book discussion groups and journal writing workshops for teens and adults. Amy lives in Tonawanda, NY with her husband and two daughters. She is an avid kayaker. This is her first published collection of poems. She can be reached at achristman@adelphia.net.

Resources

Center for Journal Therapy
Kathleen Adams LPC, RPT-MS, Director
1115 Grant Street #207, Denver CO 80203
303-986-6460   888-421-2298
www.journaltherapy.com   KAdamsRPT@aol.com
The Center for Journal Therapy is an international organization
dedicated to making the healing art of journal writing accessible to
all who desire self-directed change. Programs include home-study
Instructor Certification Training to teach the Journal to the Self
workshop. A network of Certified Instructors teach journal
workshops in many states, cities and regions in the US, Canada,
Europe and New Zealand. The Center also offers a two-year
structured local (Denver metro) or distance learning program that
meets the training requirements for the Certified Poetry/Journal
Therapist (CPT) credential. Kathleen Adams offers workshops,
training, consultation, on-line courses and individual and group
facilitation. All programs are approved for continuing education
through the National Board for Certified Counselors (NBCC).
Call or e-mail for more information.

National Association for Poetry Therapy
866-844-NAPT
www.poetrytherapy.org   NAPTStarr@aol.com
An energetic, world-wide community of people who share a love for
the use of language arts in growth and healing. Membership is
multidisciplinary. Approximately 25% are mental health
professionals, 25% doctors, nurses and physical health care
professionals, 25% educators and librarians, 25% writers and poets.
Credentialing program is available resulting in Certified

Poetry/Journal Therapist (adult education/developmental level) or Registered Poetry/Journal Therapist (clinical level). Dues are $110/year. Publications include quarterly *Journal of Poetry Therapy* and thrice-yearly *Museletter.* Annual conferences are held in April or May of each year at locations throughout the United States.

Other Books and Works by Kathleen Adams

Journal to the Self: 22 Paths to Personal Growth, 1990, Warner Books, New York. A comprehensive book featuring a technique approach to journal writing with emphasis on the therapeutic and healing aspects of reflective writing.

Journal to the Self Audio Workshop, 1994, Center for Journal Therapy, Denver CO. The complete workshop, facilitated by Kathleen Adams with a live audience. 5 cassette tapes.

Journal to the Self Workbook, 2002, Center for Journal Therapy, Denver CO. A workbook that accompanies the book and workshop.

The Way of the Journal, 2nd Ed. 1998, Sidran Press, Lutherville MD. A self-paced journal therapy workbook featuring an approach that helps structure and contain writing without imposing limitations. Especially helpful for those who have had difficulty starting or staying with a journal program, those in recovery for psychological or physical trauma, and those in psychotherapy or counseling programs.

The Write Way to Wellness: A Workbook for Healing & Change, 2000, Center for Journal Therapy. "A map for understanding body, mind and spirit." (Dana Reynolds). This workbook provides clear, expert guidance along a healing journey of self-discovery.

The Healing Fountain: Poetry Therapy for Life's Journey, 2003, NorthStar Press, St. Paul MN. Co-author (with Stephen Rojcewicz, MD, RPT) of Chapter 1, "Mindfulness on the Journey Ahead."

Professional Training

Journal to the Self Instructor Certification Training (ICT). Distance-learning self-paced study that prepares applicants to increase income by offering journal workshops in their own communities.

Certified Poetry/Journal Therapist (CPT) Program. Two-year structured program designed to meet training requirements for the Certified Poetry/Journal Therapist designation. Qualified mental health professionals may continue on for Registered Poetry/Journal Therapist (RPT) designation. Local (Denver) and distance-learning programs available.

Counselor Continuing Education. A comprehensive selection of face-to-face, home-study and Internet-based programs in journal and poetry therapy, approved for continuing education for LPCs, NCCs, and other licensed mental health professionals by the National Board of Certified Counselors (NBCC).

For more information, visit www.journaltherapy.com or contact the Center for Journal Therapy, 1115 Grant Street #207, Denver CO 80203. Phone: 303-986-6460 or 888-421-2298.